I KNOW YOU HEAR ME.
ARE YOU LISTENING?

The Empowerment of Mindful Listening™

CAROL MCCALL, PHD

AND

TUCK SELF

Hardcover: 978-1-64184-062-0
Paperback: 978-1-64184-063-7
Ebook: 978-1-64184-064-4

CONTENTS

DEDICATION

This book is dedicated to God, my son Raleigh my daughter, Ana and grand daughter Daria plus the many global citizens who have contributed to the inspiration of my mission to create 200,000,000 masterful listeners for the decade 2020.

PREFACE

LISTENING is the single most important component in communication that you and I do. Yet, LISTENING is the least practiced component in communication. The rarest component in communication is Empowered Mindful Listening™.

What is Empowered Mindful Listening™? It is the ability to listen with all four quadrants of oneself. The four quadrants are the mental quadrant, the physical quadrant, the emotional quadrant and the spiritual (intuitive) quadrant.

Imagine the possibilities when one is present and communicating with all four quadrants in operation in all relationships, in work, in family, in every area of one's life. I assert that the practice of Empowered Mindful Listening™ is becoming the next evolutionary leap for humankind. The practice of Empowered Mindful Listening™ provides an exponential impact and richness that lasts a lifetime. The practice of Empowered Mindful Listening™ provides breakthroughs, transformation and the emergence of the "mature self" (a term used by Deepak Chopra, M.D. and Rudolph E. Tanzi PhD. in their book *Super Brain*).

"Practice Makes Permanent"- author unknown

The genesis of this book occurred in a conversation with a close colleague and friend, Tuck Self. We are choosing to share our thoughts, insights and information in dialog form in order to include the reader in the conversation.

Books are special in that they allow the reader to proceed at their desired pace, to pause and ponder, to practice new concepts and to slowly begin the evolution of authenticity, the "mature self".

Our commitment to you, the reader, is that through the practice of Empowered Mindful Listening™, your evolution brings the world closer to peace, satisfaction, authenticity and completion.

"Completion is the Allness of the Universe"

~Elizabeth Claire Prophet

#1

BREVITY

SUMMATION-A SPEAKING STYLE THAT MAKES THE POINT CONCISELY AND CLEARLY.

Carol McCall, PhD: I like the idea that The Nine Tools of Empowered Mindful Listening™ are similar to *The Four Agreements* by Don Miguel Ruiz. The Nine Tools of Empowered Mindful Listening™ are the basis of the work that I do. I think basing a book on The Nine Tools of Empowered Mindful Listening™ gives people a foundation to Empowered Mindful Listening™ tools. I really embrace "the thought" of The Nine Tools of Empowered Mindful Listening™. That's not the title of the book and yet it is a good concept to build the book around.

Tuck: It's interesting as I'm listening to you. I believe that *The Four Agreements* are powerful in how they are defined, and more importantly, in how they can be practiced and experienced. To me The Nine Tools of Empowered Mindful Listening™ truly are the Nine Agreements of Listening. They are that deep. They are not just tools. They are agreements. I remember hearing you say that the opportunity for me to be in the space of listening to someone else and have them listen to me is a beautiful moment for complete intimacy. That's deep and powerful.

Carol McCall, PhD: I like that too, The Nine Agreements of Empowered Mindful Listening™.

Tuck: The Nine Tools of Empowered Mindful Listening™ can be represented by a figure 8, a continuous flow of giving and receiving in communication. This flow creates partnership between people.

McCall: The other word that comes to me is Promise, The Nine Promises of Listening. The Nine Tools are either agreements or promises. People are already attuned to what the word "agreement" means. The tool of Brevity is "I agree to be brief." I agree to be brief as I am responding to you. Brevity requires me to speak and then "shut up" and listen.

Tuck: There are two of us in conversation. There are two of us in partnership. There are two of us in the agreement. As I am listening to you there is also an agreement with myself. I'm committing to an agreement with myself to be brief in my conversation with you. That's the figure 8 we were speaking about before that now has a whole other level of meaning.

Carol McCall, PhD: Absolutely, and that is the piece that people miss. They miss that they have an agreement with themselves, a promise to themselves. **What they require from someone else requires that they be that way with themselves.** For example, if you require strength from others, are you being strong with yourself?

Tuck: (Laughing) I don't have to answer that now do I? That's a great question.

Carol McCall, PhD: Are you being that way for you? So for me to be brief, the question is "Am I brief with myself?" The answer for me is "Yes, I am brief." Very often I will find myself having one word responses to things. You ask me a question "Are you hungry?" "Yes." I don't need to elaborate on the fact.

One of the situations I often find myself in with my daughter is that she asks me a series of questions. I discover that in her pursuit of the series of questions, she has recognized and been trained that I will give her one word answers. So, she saves up. She asks, "Mom, are you hungry? Mom would you like to go to our favorite restaurant, which is not too far from here? Is that going to be too far for you to go? Will you be able to walk there?" It's a huge series of questions.

"Are you hungry?" "Yes." "Would you like to go to the restaurant that we enjoy going to together?" "Yes." "Is that going to be too far for you to go?" "No." "Will you be able to walk from the front door to the table without any discomfort?" "Yes."

All of these are Yes/No questions. She collects all of her questions in this little bag and then hands me the bag.

Tuck: I want to share two things about my personal experience with the tool of Brevity.

One is, the Human Energy Design system (*see Glossary) which powerfully reveals our individual, unique strategy for making decisions in life. In this system, both you and I are Generators and our personal strategy is to "Respond" to life.

The Generator's strategy for responding to a brief question supports the tool of Brevity. Our strategy is to respond with a brief "Uh-huh" or "Uh-uh", from our intuition or gut rather than a long drawn out logical response from our thinking mind.

We are empowered and communication is enhanced when we respond with this brief response.

The second thing I want to share is that you, Dr. C, always respond with Brevity in both spoken and written communication. You will answer, "Yes" and "Okay". That is clear communication. It's concise. I get it.

It has been fun over the years to watch myself do MSU (Making Stuff Up: Tool #7) with your brief responses. For example, I say to myself, "Oh God, I need more information to make sure she is not mad at me." Or, "Oh God, I need to know that she really wants me."

It's so interesting how the power of one tool can bring out the lack of power and the obvious lack of agreement with another tool.

Carol McCall, PhD: Brevity brings people together. It also allows mischief, like you just talked about. When I am brief, I am also aware that this leaves a space of silence. Most people are uncomfortable with silence. They fill in the silence with their thoughts and noise.

Brevity does create mischief. What people are making up is not what's happening in silence. The only thing going on is silence.

When I know I'm in the presence of someone who is very mischievous, I will share that I require a moment of silence to think. I let them know what I am doing by saying, "Let me take a moment to gather my thoughts."

Then I can be quiet without them supposedly going off on a "merry-go-round" chase, or a nonsense search of what

I'm doing. I just shared what I am doing. I'm gathering my thoughts.

They will say, "What are you thinking about?" I will tell them, "I don't know. I haven't gathered my thoughts yet. They are still coming in. Stay tuned." Yes, people get very mischievous when you are quiet. They don't know what to do with themselves.

Tuck: What is your perspective in terms of the Brevity tool when people take me through every thought process they have? I truly have to get on their train and ride it. What has people not be brief? What's behind that?

Carol McCall, PhD: That's a great question. The answer I have consistently come to is their answer has nothing to do with me or the question. Their answer has everything to do with where they are.

If the answer is really long, it's all about them proving something. The Life Decision has taken hold. They are either doing *Not Good Enough/Better Than*, they are doing *Not Enough/Too Much* or they are doing *Not Important/Most Important/Omnipotent*. They are speaking from one of those thought forms.

Tuck: Take a minute and talk about The Life Decisions.

Carol McCall, PhD: The Life Decisions, and there are five of them, are thought forms that we develop as little people somewhere between the ages of 0 and 5.

After we come into this world, we are busy formulating how the world works, with little to no information. Unfortunately many of us continue to grow up with little to no information. The Life Decision, the thought form that we "make up", is how we believe life MUST be and we operate from this thought form.

Life Decisions come in pairs. The first life decision is *Worthless/Worth More*. The second one is *Not Worthy/Deserving/Entitled*. The third life decision is *Not Good Enough/Better Than*. The fourth one is *Not Enough/Too Much*. The fifth life decision is *Not Important/Most Important/Omnipotent*.

These are the five major thought forms that we lock ourselves into between the ages of 0 and 5. From ages 6-12 we look for evidence that what we decided between 0 and 5 is the truth.

When you decide that you are *Not Good Enough* or that you "should" be *Better Than*, then no matter how much your parents and authorities praise you, the minute you hear, "That was not good enough", you incorporate that statement into the life decision. You look for evidence. "See, you said I'm not good enough."

Then from the ages 13 to approximately 20, the adolescent and teen years, we are busy solidifying our facade using the thought forms we have chosen and are developing.

We hang out with like-minded people. As adolescents we are able to see each other's pretenses and facades since we have our own. The phrase, "It takes one to know one," describes us. Adolescents know each other really well.

Then from the ages of 20 to 30 we start to select our jobs and our livelihood based on a thought form.

Then we move into marriage and we settle down based on a thought-form, the "Go live happily ever after" thought-form.

When we talk too much and we aren't brief, we are speaking from the thought-form.

The thought-form is, as an example, "The devil made me do it". The "thought form" made me do it.

Tuck: What I am hearing you say is that we are a walking thought form.

Here is what is fascinating to me about this work and The Nine Tools of Empowered Mindful Listening™. I have a copy of your book, *Listen, There is a World Waiting to Be Heard*, in front of me that you signed in 2001. Here I sit in 2018 having been a student of this work and having had you as an incredible mentor for sixteen years. And I just got a whole other level of this work. It's fascinating. I keep understanding this work at so many different levels.

Carol McCall, PhD: I wrote an article called "The Alchemy of Listening" for my newsletter. These are two quotes from this article.

One is a quote from a man I was blessed to meet at UC Berkley, Eknath Eswaran. I had a few classes with him. He is no longer here. He was a great man.

Eknath Eswaran said, "Thoughts are things. Even though you can't hold them in your hands or see them, they are different from our usual view. Usually we consider our thoughts as immaterial. So we are not aware of how a feeling thought can affect us."

The other quote comes from Abraham, translated by Jerry and Esther Hicks.

"As you perceive something, you give birth to a thought. Now this thought thinks. Now that it exists, now that it has been conjured, now that it has been focused, now it vibrates. So, by the Law of Attraction other thoughts that are vibrationally the same will come to it. So it begins its expansion immediately."

My purpose for writing the "Alchemy of Listening" was to provide clarity to the statement that we are always listening to our thoughts. You are not seeing your thoughts; you are "listening" to them.

If I throw a beach ball at you, it won't hurt you much. After 5 minutes you will have forgotten about it.

However if I say something harsh to you, you will not be able to forget that thought. You are still "listening" to that thought. You'll take it home. You'll have nightmares about it. You'll wake up oppressed the next morning.

We know from personal experience how a harsh comment from a parent or friend can rankle in our consciousness for years.

I have an associate who still holds a grudge for something I said 25 years ago. This is the immense power of thought. They have been listening to that thought for the last 25 years.

Tuck: It's a challenge for me to convey the depth of what listening is for me.

I am listening to you and know the work and the research you are getting ready to do. Quantum physics, energy and multi-dimensional listening fascinate me.

I believe that my cells are always listening and responding. My energy is always listening and responding.

As I am listening to you and responding, I'm re-discovering the evolutionary power of the Life Decision made between the ages of 0 and 5 to limit our lives.

Your body of work and how you teach listening isn't like a typical corporate course that I have attended. I have gone to classes on active and passive listening as a duty or assignment, something I have to do.

Whereas, what I have learned from you, and what I adore and am passionate about this work, is its "beingness" focus. Your body of work is the full gestalt. It provides a focus for speaking into and listening from all 4 quadrants of multi-dimensional listening.

Carol McCall, PhD: When you are listening, **all 4 quadrants are affected, mental, physical, emotional and spiritual.** You get the full gestalt, the full experience of another human being when you are listening.

Tuck: Imagine being a child again, between the ages of 0 and 5.

Carol McCall, PhD: Yes, when all 4 quadrants are wide open.

Tuck: And then you begin to collect evidence between 6 and 12 emotionally and intellectually.

Carol McCall, PhD: And spiritually. Then you go and hang out in your little cliques where you are all listening the same way. We are all having the same kind of thought forms. That's how we get into our little cliques.

Tuck: I have this conversation with you and I have it with my friends. Sometimes I feel like we are the dead walking. Many teachers say this too, that 99% of what we do we do on autopilot. How do we get out of all of this? How do we begin?

Carol McCall, PhD: We practice. We practice Brevity. You can't be brief and be absent. You can't be brief and be in the past and the future. **Brevity requires you to be focused and present in the moment, right now, so you can be brief.**

How do you get out of autopilot listening? The answer is not to start. I'm not saying that the Life Decision will not start.

A long-time associate of mine sent me a Facebook picture of his new born son. He was not even a week old. This baby is looking at the camera. I got it. He is here. He is present. He is focused at 3 days. He is looking at the camera. There isn't this glazed over look like he doesn't know what he is looking at. He is here.

I said, "Welcome. Hello." He is very present. The father wrote back, "Yes, he is very focused."

This was an amazing thing to see. Children are focused. Between the ages of 0 and 5 they are focused.

Tuck: The question I want to ask is where are they focused? Is it here?

Carol McCall, PhD: They are focused on the moment. They are focused on whatever is happening in the moment. They are not anywhere except here. Those babies and those children are in full gear; mental, physical, emotional and spiritual. They are present in the moment with what is going on.

This is where parents have challenges from the perspective that when the moment changes, so do children. This moment has their attention now. And this next moment has their attention because the moments are changing. So, they are going with the moment.

Tuck: I have 2 epiphanies.

In the world that we live in today and in this time of Great Change there is conversation around being present. There is conversation around expanding our human form for conscious awareness. There is conversation about all the dimensions, physical, emotional, mental and spiritual.

People are looking for how to be aware of and integrate the 4 quadrants. They are looking for how to expand and be alive and live in those 4 quadrants.

I know I ask this question year after year, "What does it mean to be present?" I'm looking at the Nine Tools while I'm listening to you, and I'm seeing how deeply powerful they are.

The Nine Tools of Empowered Mindful Listening™ are the wave of the future. They are a beautiful pathway to being present.

The Nine Tools of Empowered Mindful Listening™ are the experience of being present in all 4 quadrants to yourself, the person you are in conversation with and God.

That is quite cool. It's powerful, the simplicity of knowing you have 9 agreements. It might not be easy but the tools are simple.

Carol McCall, PhD: It's absolutely simple. These tools have the ability to transmute, not only transform. They transmute.

Tuck: I'm so excited right now. I'm going to take a copy of these Nine Tools and post them like the Four Agreements, so that I am aware and can practice. It's important to know how to integrate this into my being. How can I "be" these tools?

Carol McCall, PhD: The question is not how can you "be" these tools. The question is how do you *access* the tools? You already are the tools. You are *Being*. In Being, that question is an oxymoron. You are really asking how you can "do" Being? You don't because you already *are* the tools. When you accept that you are these tools you won't ask the question how you could "be" them. You already are.

Tuck: Well that question certainly makes sense when I'm coming from the Life Decision of Not Good Enough/Better Than. The Life Decision was certainly present with me a moment ago when you corrected me. I thought, "How dare she correct me, I'm Better Than that."

Carol McCall, PhD: You already *are* these tools. Now how do you access them? Be present and focus on this particular moment. When you shared with me, "How dare she correct me?" In that particular moment you became present to what was there for you. You spoke your truth, which brought you back to this particular conversation and back to being focused and present. The Life Decision was gone when you spoke your truth. The moment you speak of the boogey man, he is gone. There is no boogey man in the present moment.

So how do you access who you already "be"? Be present. Well, how do you "be" present? That's like asking how do you do presence? You know how to be present. You focus. Everybody knows how to be. They focus!

Tuck: The other word that comes up for me when you say focus is silence. There is power in silence. I wrote myself a note to suggest that when you are writing your blog post that a beautiful post would be, "Are you comfortable with Silence?"

Carol McCall, PhD: Many people cannot stand the silent moments. I treasure when my daughter and I take trips

I KNOW YOU HEAR ME. ARE YOU LISTENING?

together. We can ride for long periods of time and not say a word, and we love being with each other. We don't say a word. It's wonderful. Then there are also times when the Life Decision pops up and says, "Okay enough of this."

Tuck: It's time for a little drama.

I'm looking at the definition of Brevity and the word that continues to come up is clarity. I know we are talking about listening. When I look at the word clarity and feel into it, it has a visual component to me. I "see" clearly when I listen with Brevity. There is an internal vision that provides the clarity for me.

Carol McCall, PhD: I got feedback from a prospective client yesterday in her 30-minute complimentary coaching session. My question was, "What are you taking away from this call?" She said, "Clarity." I asked, "What was the clarity about?" She said, "Well, you were concise, direct, and you had me answer the question without going into the unasked for explanation. What I got was the simplicity of answering a question, simply answering the question without any garnishment. You asked me the question, 'How do you like your hotdog?' I said, 'Plain.' You said, 'Okay.' You didn't say, 'Wouldn't you like some relish, mustard, ketchup, pickles and onions?' You didn't ask me any of that. You asked me, 'How do you like your hotdog?' And I said, 'Plain.' That's clear. I also experienced acceptance." She said, "So I'm leaving with clarity, acceptance and actions in relationship to my son."

Brevity allows for exactly what you said, clarity. It's concise.

Tuck: Your client used a word that triggers people and that word is direct. I was going to ask you about being direct in the definition of Brevity. The way that direct is being used here means focus and presence. Brevity is getting to the bottom line. You were direct when you gave your prospective client feedback. Sometimes people look at directness as if it is coming from a Type A personality and that there is something wrong with being direct.

Carol McCall, PhD: We are encouraged at a very early age, somewhere between 0 and 5 not to say things. How often do you hear parents say to children, "Don't say that!"? We learn to camouflage. We learn to lie, by omission, about our truth.

We can give a direct answer to how much something cost. It cost $20. Rather than, "Well it didn't cost much. It won't break your pocket book if you buy this." I didn't ask you this. I asked, "How much does it cost?"

Tuck: Listening is fun.

Carol McCall, PhD: It is. I'm proud to share that my daughter and I finished our taxes and are getting them in on time. She was explaining something to me. As I was listening to her I realized she wasn't talking to me. She was explaining something for herself. I listened from the perspective of it is okay to let her do this. This isn't about me. This is about her. I listened. Then I thanked her.

Tuck: In the beginning of this conversation we talked about listening in partnership and in all 4 quadrants. As I pictured you and your daughter talking, I got the image of the Figure 8. Where you do something for the other person, you do it for yourself. When you do something for yourself, you do it for the other.

We have been talking today and I've been taking notes. The word benefit keeps coming up for me. What is the value and benefit of listening? Earlier I spoke about being present to listening to and from all 4 quadrants. The two words I added when I was listening to you were acceptance and empathy. That's huge. You were with your daughter. She felt acceptance and empathy. See how excited I get? This is huge.

Carol McCall, PhD: Brevity is a very powerful tool. I appreciated what you said earlier that as you spend more and more time with these tools, Brevity helps access the 4 quadrants. When you are brief, and when I am brief, I am available to listen to you with all 4 quadrants wide open, all 4 cylinders wide open. I said what I had to say. I can "get" all parts of you- mental, physical, emotional, and spiritual.

It's uncomfortable for people to have that kind of undivided listening. You have my full listening, which is what we all crave. We all do. It's a sense of belonging. We are all looking for somewhere to belong. It's that interdependence we look for. Empowered Mindful Listening™ provides that.

You've heard it many times before. We are all one. We are all part of each other. My inner critic, the human ego with me loves to keep itself separate from others and says, "I'm not part of you." So I say to the human ego, "Well, yes, you are. There are parts of your behavior where I don't do them like you do them. And I do ask myself the question, what's **my** version of that behavior? I don't have your behaviors...and... what does my version of that behavior look like?"

Am I okay with my version of that behavior? Does it serve me? If the answer is yes, that's good. If the answer is no, I change it. I don't always change it quickly.

I have a blanket like Linus. I will put any other blanket on top of that one to stay warm. That one has to stay near my body. Any time I use any other blanket I don't sleep well. The minute I put this one on, the touch of it sends me off to a sound sleep. If I get cold I can put something on top of this one. It amuses me that I love this blanket. The only time I wash it is during the day when I am not on it.

Where does all of this come from? What am I listening to? The truth is I'm very brief. I'm brief with my blanket. I get it into the wash. I get it out and onto the bed.

Tuck: I'm trying to remember where I heard a statement. It was at the time around the movie *The Secret*. It was, "Whatever I'm listening for is what I'm listening from."

Carol McCall, PhD: When you are listening from something you miss the total message.

Tuck: Because you have your filter.

Carol McCall, PhD: Yes you are listening from a filter.

Tuck: I had this thought about the TV show *The Voice*. I thought wouldn't it be fun to have a show like this around listening? The judges are listening without any interference from the physicality. They are listening with the ear. What would we call our show?

Carol McCall, PhD: Ah I got it. There is the voice. Then there are the ears, and the heart. The heart is commonly used. Many people pretend to listen from the heart. There is no new show coming, yet. There is the show called *The Listener*. It's a drama show. It is an interesting show. The lead character solves murder mysteries. He hears people's thoughts and listens. He says he reads their minds. He is listening.

Tuck: The reason I love the Nine Tools is because they are simple. I have done your work. I have worked with Christian Pankhurst and his beautiful community of Heart Intelligence. That's what part of that work does as well. People sit in a circle.

They listen to one another and give feedback energetically on what they are hearing and feeling.

We don't sit in workshops every day. We are out in the world engaged, working jobs and in relationships. To be able to have these tools accessible, to me, is a gift to people.

I have been in workshops with you. I have seen you sit in front of people in the room and do the same thing that the judges do on The Voice, listening. I had that picture in my mind of this extraordinary show with the chairs and us listening and then turning around. It is a fascinating concept.

Carol McCall, PhD: It would be a great show in terms of having it be a talk show with one group of people facing the audience, and the judges with their backs to the people talking. The judges determine who is authentic and who is not in terms of what they have to say.

Tuck: Do you remember, since we are of a certain age, the TV show *To Tell the Truth*? It had Kitty Carlisle. Three people would come out and each would say, "I am Bill Smith." They would ask each of them questions to determine who was the real Bill Smith and who were the imposters. So we have the show *The Voice* and we have the new show *The Talk*. We may be onto something Dr. C.

Carol McCall, PhD: We might be.

Tuck: For now, in this moment, we are going over The Nine Tools of Empowered Mindful Listening™. Is there anything else to say about Brevity?

Carol McCall, PhD: (Sigh). No, I think we have been brief enough.

Tuck: I love your sigh. That was very brief. Brevity is in the sigh.

Carol McCall, PhD: I am complete.

Tuck: Completion is good. It is also a tool. It is Tool #8 in The Nine Tools of Empowered Mindful Listening™.

#2

ACKNOWLEDGEMENT

A SPEAKING STYLE THAT ENHANCES THE COMMUNICATION IN THE FORM OF CONTRIBUTION.

Tuck: I prepared for today's conversation by reading the tool of Acknowledgement in your book, *Listen, There is a World Waiting to be Heard.*

Carol McCall, PhD: What did you get in terms of what you read?

Tuck: What I got this time that I didn't get before was the focus on "agenda", particularly when using acknowledgement in a corporate environment, and how it supports the overall win-win. I have allowed my personal insecurities to get in the way and have not stayed present.

I'm clear my intention is to support and encourage others. My tendency has been to question myself going into a conversation with a personal agenda. When I have an agenda I have the thought that I am driving and/or manipulating the conversation rather than being open to what can emerge in the interaction.

What I got this time as I reread this tool was how having an agenda can support the person I am in conversation with and move the team toward an intended outcome.

I got that being specific with my agenda and supporting the individual through an Acknowledgement creates an environment where we are in partnership around the intended outcome.

I'm eager for today's conversation to gauge my interpretation of this particular tool.

Carol McCall, PhD: That piece around agenda has been so far removed from my current thinking about Acknowledgment. It has morphed for me in terms of agenda.

My initial intention for Acknowledgment was to validate the speaker and let the speaker know what I had done with what they said, in terms of how their message contributed to me in the interchange.

It has been my experience for so many years that people speak and others are listening, and yet the speaker doesn't even know what's being done with what's being said.

How are you receiving what was said? How are you interpreting it? What are the feelings you have when you hear what I say? What are you making up when you hear what I say?

The Acknowledgment piece came up to resolve those questions.

The meaning of Acknowledgment is morphing into meaning BEING KNOWN. This taps into a conversation you and I had a couple of days ago

When I acknowledge you, it is to let you know that you are known. When I acknowledge you it's to let you know your message landed in such a way that I now KNOW you. You experience being known.

I say that the REAL hunger in the world is that people want to be known. People take "selfies", pictures of themselves, because they want to be known.

Having fame, even for 15 seconds, is about being known. It's having a sense of "somebody out there knows me". My existence counts. It's about being known.

I'm excited to discover the different layers of the tool of Acknowledgement. For example, what else does Acknowledgement do for people; how does Acknowledgement nourish people?

When you acknowledge me Tuck, I fully experience an expansion within myself. One of the things celebrities feed off of is Acknowledgement.

The bigger the crowd is the bigger the expansion. The very aura of that performer gets brighter and brighter. They feed off of that kind of Acknowledgement. It's important for them to know that they do exist and that they count for something.

I think one of the most successful and prolific managers of Acknowledgement is Kim Kardashian. She came from literally fixing people's closets to being a universal celebrity. Everybody around the globe knows who Kim Kardashian is.

What did she start with? Not much! However, she made sure that she was known. Now she is known.

It is very useful to watch how people manipulate, and I use that word deliberately. They manipulate time and energy to be known. People are hungry to be known.

So that is my thought about Acknowledgment today.

Your agenda piece that you brought up it's like oh, yeah. There is that part to Acknowledgement that I have morphed from. For you to bring it back into my awareness has me understand that now we are talking about layers of Acknowledgement.

It depends on where people are in terms of how they will hear the Acknowledgement, how they will ingest it and what they will do with it.

I'm thanking you for reminding me that this has to do with where people are in terms of Acknowledgment.

There will still be people who can't accept Acknowledgement. They will shoo it away. They will dismiss or diminish it. They can't be with Acknowledgement and yet that is the very thing they hunger for. So that's my thought about Acknowledgment.

Tuck: I want to go back to our conversation the other day around the book, *The Four Agreements* by Don Miguel Ruiz. The 2nd Agreement is "Don't Take Anything Personally". The 2nd Agreement instructs us not to take negative feedback personally as well as positive feedback received in the form of an Acknowledgment.

However, when I receive an Acknowledgment, for example, "Tuck I really appreciate the contribution you made to me," I feel known, seen and heard.

What's the distinction between taking that feedback personally and receiving the contribution? I might be collapsing something here, so would you speak about that for a minute?

Carol McCall, PhD: Don't take it personally that your presence has contributed to that person's expansion. You have shown up, said something, and your energy has impacted that person.

You have demonstrated the energy of Interdependence. In that moment of Acknowledgement you have become interdependent with that person. You have aligned with that person's energy.

We acknowledged them so they get who they are themselves. Our only participation was that we showed up. We said whatever it was that we said. It really doesn't have anything to do with us in terms of the ego snatching it up and saying, "Look what I did."

I'm clear that the Four Agreements are NOT ego driven. They are SPIRIT driven. Spirit doesn't take credit. "Don't take it personally" means don't take credit for what you did for another person.

Tuck: It's interesting. I believe I've heard you say before, that in the moment of interacting, when we are present to one another, we are receiving what they are giving. The lines are blurred. The presence of that moment is one of beauty and power.

When it is over I snatch it away. The ego snatches it away. That's the point of the whole listening thing. Once I decide to describe Presence and/or talk about it, I am no longer in the present moment.

The two things I wrote down as you were sharing were 1) don't take things personally and the other that kept coming up was about 2) the self-obsession and narcissism of the ego for wanting to be fed.

I understand the distinction now. **When I am in the present moment receiving Acknowledgment I am expanded. I feel heard.** It is completely different than taking the Acknowledgment and feeding my ego. It's quite subtle, almost too subtle for conversation.

Carol McCall, PhD: It requires each of us to be at a level of listening where you can hear the subtlety even if you don't have the words to describe it. Energetically you get it.

For me to find the words to convey to you, that's when the little ego comes in to try and size it up, package it up to sound a certain way. The whole point is missed. The little bitty ego is not equipped to describe something that magnificent and of that magnitude.

That's what a quantum is. It's so tiny that it shifts the entire Universe. People think a quantum is a huge thing and yet it is very subtle. It literally makes a world of difference.

The quantum is about the subtle. It is so subtle that the ego misses it. It misses the subtlety because it is being intellectual. It's too subtle for the ego to "get it".

Think about it this way. The earth moves on its axis. If there is the slightest movement away from its axis we would all be in trouble. That's the level at which we need to listen and need to be subtle. It's of that magnitude.

When people get that being interdependent is not a scary thing, it's actually a form of expansion. There is more to us when we are interdependent. There is more of us to be available.

On the one hand I'm glad that people have not gotten this one yet. It means I'll be in business for a while. That's good news.

The other good news is what an exciting opening and presence this understanding brings, what an exciting vision and dynamic to watch.

Yesterday a very sad event happened in my life, and yet I was able to acknowledge myself so I expanded out of that sad experience. I was able to acknowledge an aspect of myself.

Now the ego wanted to come in and snatch it up.

However, in terms of the Acknowledgment, in terms of the greater part of me, not the ego itself, I felt compassion. Even in the sadness of the moment, and the moment was a harsh one, there was compassion that the moment had occurred.

How I perceived the moment had everything to do with my expansion. I could've perceived the moment as, "Look at what they did to me," and taken it personally. Yet, I had an experience of my own expansion as I spoke about my sadness.

I was able to see that incident from a place of compassion even though it was intended to have brought harm and pain to me. I saw the source of it as in, "Oh My Gosh!"

I saw how terrified this person must have been to have done that. I saw the depth of the fear and the ugliness that person lives in. In that moment I had compassion.

As I was discussing it, I experienced hatred. Yet in the moment of hatred, I also experienced compassion. This person is in hatred, and still if they were lying in a ditch bleeding to death, I might walk past, and as I walked past I would dial 911.

Their reaction to me was a 911 call. This person needs help, even in the face of their viciousness.

This moment was very powerful. I acknowledged myself. Now coming full circle, I feel known by me, not by anybody else but by myself. I know me.

I know I would not leave this person to die in the ditch. I would call 911. I might not help them; however, I would call 911.

Calling 911 is my version of turning the other cheek. "Whatever you do to the least of us, you do to me" was Christ's statement. I would call 911 for Christ. That's the Christ within me.

I don't have to worry about me becoming that harsh and having that level of terror. Recognizing that Christ is in me is an Acknowledgement. I'm known. Most importantly, I am known to me.

Tuck: When I was in contemplation this morning and reading the 2nd Agreement about not taking things personally, I was reminded of something you said to me the other day about interdependency.

I am on an evolutionary journey in accepting myself the way I am and truly knowing myself. When I come to the conversation from the space of truly knowing myself, we'll both experience that level of presence.

I have the thought that you and I have merged. We are witnessing and co-creating together. At this moment in time we are evolving, individually and in partnership together. We are each other's evolutionary witness. It's a journey for each of us.

Carol McCall, PhD: I have the thought that each one of us is our own Dalai Lama and Eckhart Tolle. The distinction between them and us is that we haven't come to that level of acceptance, where we completely slough off the veil, the ego. We haven't come to that yet. That's part of the journey.

I've had brief moments of sloughing off the veil and the ego. It is awesome to experience myself in the fullness of the true self, the God self. There is total and complete humility, like we see in Pharrell Williams. It's a level of humility and gratefulness.

To have moments like this is to be known to myself. To be known to myself not having an ego supports me in knowing that I'm okay! I no longer have to live in the space of, "Oh no! I'm going to be found out as an imposter."

There are actions and behaviors that I exhibit that are counter indicative to the real me, to my real self. That's the imposter.

Who I really am is not an imposter. However, a lot of times my behavior is definitely false. It is not true to who I am.

We've had conversations where, for example, you said to me, "You probably think I'm [fill in the blank]."

I said, "No, I know you. The behaviors and actions you take are the things you do when you are not present. You are known by me. When you are present Tuck, I know you. You are bubbly. You are a cheerleading team all by yourself. You can't help it. You just cheer. You are a walking cheer. That's the true you."

27

Tuck: That's so good Dr. C, because actually I was never able to jump in the air with split legs like cheerleaders.

Carol McCall, PhD: You are the one that's tossed up in the air and the gang catches you, and then they put you back down.

You are the one that gets the crowd to do the wave. You lead the wave.

I have the experience that you don't place yourself there often, in terms of your ground of being, and that being a cheerleader is your core self.

Tuck: Wow, in that moment as I was listening, I was aware that the mind is so quick. I had to shift myself from thinking about what you were saying to fully letting it in.

Carol McCall, PhD: Yes, you were shifting in that moment and becoming interdependent. You were becoming one with the communication and the words that were coming in. You ingested what was being said rather than analyzing what was said.

A lot of people are ANALyzing what is being said when they are listening.

They are trying to figure out what something means rather than ingesting what is being said. They miss the full gestalt and taste of what is being spoken.

Tuck: At the beginning of the call you were speaking about communication and you said something profound.

You said if we are in conversation, what is really important in the communication is not so much what I am saying to you, but what you are doing with what I am saying to you. How are you interpreting it? What are the feelings you have when you hear what I say? What are you making up with what I say?

When I'm in a conversation, my habit is to worry rather than ask you what you did with what I said. I worry rather than truly being present and listening. How does someone get out of this space?

Carol McCall, PhD: Are you willing to practice asking the questions, "What are you doing with what I just said? What did you get out of what I just shared?" Put these questions in the space.

This way you begin to trust that two things are going on. Number one is that you intuitively got that the listener did indeed ingest the message rather than analyze the message. You take yourself out of your head by asking the question and finding out.

Get out of your head. Become present and ask the question, "What are you doing with what I just said?"

Number two is you find out how they heard what you said. Make sure they don't parrot your message. It is important to know how they are receiving your message and what they did with what you said.

Ask them, "I want to know how you are using what I just said. Are you using it? Did you get something out of it?"

Tuck: That goes back to my question about the agenda in the very beginning of our conversation. These two questions support the clarity of any conversation around the agenda.

Carol McCall, PhD: It's okay to have an agenda. I have a client who has done a lot of personal growth work. She says about 15 years.

Tuck: Is her name Tuck Self? (Laugh)

Carol McCall, PhD: Her agenda, in terms of Acknowledgement, is that everything she does is done with the intention of being acknowledged. For example, "Look how good I was. Look how early I showed up today."

My agenda for acknowledging her is with the understanding that she is like this little hungry bird in her nest, with her mouth wide open waiting to be fed one worm at a time.

My agenda is to feed her one Acknowledgement at a time and to gradually wean her from the need to constantly be acknowledged.

One of her homework assignments was to write down 5 things she would like to be acknowledged for at the end of the day. She is also to keep an Acknowledgement journal.

The person who doesn't acknowledge her is herself. That's how come I say it's okay to have an agenda for Acknowledgment. It's especially supportive for those who can't hear Acknowledgement.

I also have a male client who shares with me ten things he is satisfied with himself within the first few minutes of our call.

He is challenged to acknowledge himself so having the agenda to do so is helpful. It's hard at first and gets easier by the time he gets to ten. His energy has shifted because he is taking the time to acknowledge himself.

That's an agenda in terms of Acknowledgment. It's a very powerful listening tool. It's important to place it at the appropriate level. For me it is level 101.

Interdependence is at the PhD level. It is subtle and powerful when you use acknowledgement in terms of experiencing your own expansion, as being known to yourself. That is an entirely new level. It's a transformational and powerful tool. So as far as our level of use with others, we are using level 101.

Acknowledgment takes on an entirely new dynamic as we continue to grow and expand and be known to ourselves.

It's what I have experienced with the Dalai Lama and Eckhart Tolle. It's pure humility. There is no arrogance, simply pure humility.

Tuck: This is such a small moment but I remember it profoundly.

My mom and I used to watch the Miss America contest. Sometime in the sixties, the contestants were given a list of words and asked to choose a word that was most important and vital to one's character.

The winner that year chose the word humility. I remember my mom being quite moved by the fact that she chose that particular word.

It's a huge concept we are talking about, "being known to one self." Part of that statement feels familiar inside of me and then there is a part that feels unfamiliar.

Carol McCall, PhD: I have often said and will continue to say, YOU (generic you) are the most fascinating and interesting person you will ever meet. The more you know you, the more the world will benefit from you.

I'm going to be on a panel this month. It is part of the International Listening Association. It's the National Communication Association.

This is their 100th year of being in business. They started in 1914. It was an association of teachers in public speaking. That is how it started. It began here in Chicago.

As a result of being invited to participate at this convention, I was inspired to do my brain wave research.

I'm not willing to simply TALK about listening. I'm not ever tired of talking about it; however, it is the antithesis of listening.

You don't talk about listening. You listen. You listen to listening.

I have 5 minutes on the panel. I have done a lot of preparation for those 5 minutes.

At first the ego wanted to play with the fact that I only had 5 minutes to talk about listening. Then, I realized the invitation was not designed for my 5 minutes. It was to launch the brain wave research. That was the purpose. So even if I have 5 minutes I have accomplished my purpose.

To become known as one of the researchers who is now using brain wave research to study listening and to validate and give credibility to listening, to be on the cutting edge of this, is right on purpose.

I am a pioneer. I'm supposed to do this. So, it wasn't about being on the panel. It's what happened as a result of being invited to be on the panel.

Tuck: I'm excited for you. I have my pom-poms out.

Carol McCall, PhD: Because of this invitation, we are moving into Phase Two with our Brain Wave Research. We have completed Phase One of our testing.

We have started our testing to see the effect listening has on brain waves, to know what part of the brainwaves are being impacted by listening- delta, theta, gamma.

What do I want others to know? How do I want to be known? How do I want to be acknowledged? To be discovered. Stay tuned.

#3

EMPOWERED MINDFUL LISTENING™

A LISTENING STYLE THAT "SERVES" BOTH SPEAKER AND LISTENER.

Carol McCall, PhD: In The Listening Institute, formerly The Institute for Global Listening and Communication, we offer 2 workshops. One is the Empowered Mindful Listening™ workshop* and the other is The Possibility of Woman workshop now called the Advanced Women's Intensive*. (*see Glossary)

Depending on which workshop we are facilitating, there are 3 or 5 Tools of Empowered Mindful Listening™.

In The Empowered Mindful Listening™ workshop we have 5 tools: Leadership, Capability, Respect, Partnership and Cooperation. In the Advanced Women's Intensive there are 3 tools: Leadership, Capability and Respect.

One of the first components of Empowered Mindful Listening™ is capability.

What is important, as I think of my son, is capability. I am holding him as capable to live his life as he needs to live it at this phase of his life, as he matures. He is in transition, research, review and reflection. He has recently passed the 50 year mark. He is not where he anticipated himself to be.

I am not where I thought I would be in my seventies. In fact, where we are is not where any one of us thought we'd be at this phase of our lives.

Welcome to transition.

Are we capable of making it through? Can we bounce back? The answer is yes.

Whatever structures I've used in the past to bounce back, while I've used them effectively, now I'm to expand on them. I'm to expand even more. This comes as a surprise to me. There is more for me to expand. I'm aware and engaged with my hesitation in my expansion.

I'm up for it. When I recently received news about my ex-husband's physical condition, I had the thought about my own mortality.

When I presence myself in the time continuum, my being here is like the blink of an eye. While I am here, what am I going to do that makes a difference? What was I sent here to do? Am I doing that? Am I pretending to do something or am I really doing something?

Am I going to make myself uncomfortable? Am I "capable" of making myself uncomfortable? Holding myself as capable has been an interesting perspective. When I hold myself as capable the possibilities are endless. Am I going to hold myself as capable?

Tuck: So what is it that we tend to worry or have anxiety about around the capability of others?

I have children. The question I ask myself is can I hold my now adult children as capable of living his or her own life? Can I treat them with respect?

I tend to worry about everyone. Really, who is it that I'm worrying about?

As I think about you getting this work out into the world, I always go to the place of thinking about the essence of listening and the impact it can have on the world.

What is the essence of capability? What is the essence of respect? What is the essence of experiencing yourself with leadership? What is the essence of you experiencing yourself in partnership and cooperation with yourself, others and God?

There are "in power" and "out of power" needs of the ego for power, safety and value.

I make up that I use the "out of power" ways to feel safe in the world because of my neediness, attachment to things and preoccupation with control. This keeps me from listening and being present. However, when I am present I listen with respect and capability.

How can we listen to one another with capability, leadership, respect, partnership and cooperation and produce your book?

So I'm listening. I'll shut up now.

Carol McCall, PhD: When you talk about how we hold ourselves "in power", I'm having the thought that I know I made a promise to do something. When I look at how poorly

I stick to my promises I go back to a very early memory. I go back to the past and that's where "in power" or "out of power" needs of the ego show up.

I remember when I determined not to keep my word. I remember that distinctly. It happened around the time 2 children were murdered. There was one who was kidnapped and murdered by two boys. The second was a child murdered in Mississippi. In the first incident, where a child was kidnapped and murdered, the murderers studied the kidnapped child's schedule. They studied his routine.

I remember thinking that I won't stay with a routine. I won't keep my promises so that no one can nail me down or locate me. I don't want to be caught and murdered. I remember the thought. It was a trauma for me.

Here I am in my seventies and since I was 3, 4 or 5 years old, I am still impacted by that thought. I was traumatized. That experience has had everything to do with my not being empowered still today and there is less impact with that thought the longer I practice focus and presence.

The decision I made was only to go so far so that I would not be killed off. That would be the "out of power" ego making up it is "in power." The human ego in me does not want to be killed off.

I find this very interesting since I've had near death experiences. I know what it is to die and come back. Each time I wasn't interested in coming back and each time I came back as a result of the promise. This book is a step in keeping my promise. Staying out of my son's life and letting him live it is keeping my promise. It's very powerful.

Tuck: Talk to me about the tool of Empowered Mindful Listening™.

Carol McCall, PhD: Empowered Mindful Listening™ has to do with listening to oneself, so let's use me as an example.

Am I capable? Am I a leader? Do I respect what I say? The answer must be yes, since I'm in tears right now. I MUST do this. I am not driven to do this. I am compelled. I can do no other.

Right now in this moment I am in touch with my Life Purpose. This work is about serving. It is about living in a listening called capability. It's called living in a listening called respect and partnership. It's about living in a listening called cooperation. So I'm cooperating with you.

You are a manifestation of something bigger called the Universe. I'm partnering with you as a manifestation of something bigger. It is the God within you that I am partnering with as a result of a promise I made.

There is the leader in you and the leader in me. We have agreed to bring this work forth into the world. That's part of the promise. Are we capable? Absolutely.

Whether I want to or not has nothing to do with being capable. Very often I distort the two. There are times when I don't want to be capable. That does not mean I am not capable.

When I tell the truth that I **do** want to bring this work forth into the world and keep the promise, then I get busy and get back to work.

Tuck: I want you to hear this from me. This exchange is beyond deep and rich for me. I have been listening.

What I heard you say and what I did with it was this. I heard you say that you came into this world and you made a promise to do something and that you and I, in partnership and cooperation, will bring this work to fruition through The Nine Tools of Empowered Mindful Listening™.

In my listening today, I have a whole different feeling and experience of holding myself as capable. It's about listening to myself as a leader, as someone who can lead with you in the process of completing the book. It's about listening with respect to your promise enough to hold myself as capable of holding you to your promise of this completion.

It's listening to myself as a capable leader so that I treat our project with respect, and co-lead and partner with you to bring this book to fruition. It feels like a much deeper level of commitment and accountability to the completion of the book today based on the story you shared and the decision you made.

I've had a whole new experience of Empowered Mindful Listening™ today.

Carol McCall, PhD: Something has shifted. I don't know what time it was yesterday; however, I dozed off. I woke up to a woman on the entertainment news sharing that she had just had a baby. She was annoyed that she had to be more concerned about her public image than taking care of her newborn baby. She was frustrated that she had to make a choice between her image and her baby.

She said, "I am a public figure. I know, as a public figure, I have to be a role model. Whether I agree with it or not, I am and I have to be visible. I have to walk my talk. I have to reflect what it is I say I am up to."

That phrase, "I have to reflect what I say I am up to" hit me. I have to keep my promise. I have to reflect what I say I am up to.

I know I am a powerful listener. I know people change and transform when they work with me and yet there has been this question for me with the human ego and the human ego chatter.

I'm not referring to the human ego when I acknowledge the gift with which I've been blessed. I am able to listen to others and how they heal. The way that I mindfully listen is what I am committed to bringing to the world. That's my promise.

I'm not the only one. I'm not alone. I have partners.

When people really listen, there is an energetic exchange and healing that goes on when people are heard. That is the simplicity, greatness and marvel of all of it in terms of listening. All you have to do is listen. Just shut up and listen.

These days they are calling it Mindful Listening. Listening is mindful. You listen to what is going on in the moment. When you are really listening you are in the moment. There is no criticism, condemnation or judgment. You are present and in the moment.

I know the Universe is listening to different ways to return us to who we really are. Who we really are, from my perspective, are cells in the body of the Creator. Each cell has it's own job.

My job is to make sure people listen. Who are you in terms of being a cell in God's body? What is your job? What did you come here to do?

Tuck, from my perspective, you came here to cheer all of the other cells on. For me, you represent the everlasting energizer bunny. I observe that you really promote and energize, uphold and cheer people on. You come from a ground of really supporting people.

My point of view is that we are all cells in the body of God. I will make good on my promise since I said I would.

In retrospect, what kept me from keeping my promise was the 3 year old who got scared. She said if I really function as a cell I'll get murdered. That's the thought of a 3 year old and I'm letting **that** thought run my life.

It is no accident that I am moving into the Brainwave Work. This is about me literally rewiring my brain so that I can move forward to deliver on my promise.

When involved in my spiritual training with Elizabeth Claire Prophet, I recalled the thought that I had as a 3 year old who got scared that she'd be murdered.

Elizabeth talked about her husband Mark Prophet and how he rewired himself. He had been obese at one point. He was able to rewire his hypothalamus and pituitary gland and lost an enormous amount of weight.

Now she didn't call it rewiring. She did say he reinvented himself. He reorganized himself physiologically. She used the term "brain wave concentration." He used a mantra and a physical action and he went from walking to sprinting to running. She contributed much of his success to prayer, which I support.

You really can shift and work with your brain waves so that your thought patterns can shift, as long as it's followed by physical action. People who have been dealing with neuroscience and brain wave science have been doing this for a while now. I am clear I am new to the party and it makes sense to me.

Looking at the study of brain waves it does make sense to pay attention to what I am doing and how I listen. The more I understand how my own brain functions, the more I can understand how to effectively deliver on my promise of Empowered Mindful Listening™.

That's all I can say about it right now. So I'm still in research. It's still new territory to me that I haven't been into prior to now. I'm unwilling to get cerebral about it. I want to take all 4 parts with me into this arena: mental, physical, emotional and spiritual. I don't know how to do that yet.

Tuck: I have a comment. I've been listening and I am listening. I've said this before and I'll say it again. It is imperative that people hear your version, your description, your life experience and your teaching on the power of listening, and all that comes with it.

People are not listening. They are so busy "doing" their lives, struggling, in survival mode and living with effort. They are so in the meat, in the body, in the matter, in the ego and they are not listening. It doesn't matter that they are not listening out there. They're not listening to themselves.

I shared with you recently that I read a book by Sol Luckman, who is doing work in what he calls Era III of Meta-Genetics, a step beyond Epigenetics. Everyone in the epigenetic world talks about light waves and the vibrations of light. Luckman shares that what we are moving towards as a consciousness is a meta-genetic way of being, which has everything to do with sound vibration, not just light but both.

I am reading this information about the junk DNA, which is the 98% of unused DNA. We are mutating and using parts of that DNA to mutate in ways we never have before. I'm discovering that we are mutating through sound vibration.

What if we learned how to listen? What if we learned how to listen in silence? There's listening in silence.

I look at your work and want you to speak from your wisdom and your knowing and experience. I want to get these Nine Tools of Empowered Mindful Listening™ written down so that the rest of the world can read, hear, listen, experience and practice them.

There was a powerful quote in Sol Luckman's book made by Joachim-Ernst Berendt in his book, *The World is Sound*.

> "Many outstanding scholars, scientists, psychologists, philosophers and writers have described and circumscribed the New Consciousness. But one aspect has not been pointed out: that it will be the consciousness of hearing people."

To be clear Sol Luckman says, "The New Man will be a Listening Man – or will never be at all. He will be able to perceive sounds in a way we cannot even imagine today."

I believe the "new human being" will be one that knows how to listen to themselves, others and God. That's challenging work.

So, how do people listen with Empowered Mindful Listening™? Can it be described? Is it a process? Is it both?

Carol McCall, PhD: Bottom line, Empowered Mindful Listening™ is about holding yourself as capable. Do you hold yourself as capable? Do people hold themselves as capable?

I went to a convention last week. I was with a respectable panel of professors. I was quickly unattached from this body of wise professors from the perspective of listening.

When it came to my turn on the panel I opened my mouth and put my foot in it. I said, "Talking about listening is an oxymoron." That was my opening sentence. Immediately I raised feathers. People on the panel became hostile.

Talking about listening is an oxymoron. You can't talk about listening. You have to practice listening, which means keeping your mouth closed.

I'm sitting with a body of communication professors. These are individuals who go into media, social media and television and radio. I was informed that communication majors talk a lot. However, there is a component in their curriculum called listening, instead of the other way around. If they are called communication majors their major focus ought to be listening. They need to "shut up and listen."

One woman attacked me about what I had to say. I get that it was not personal. She said listening is thinking. She said that the brain has everything to do with listening because it is about thinking. This woman doesn't have the current research information that's being done around listening.

People are teaching mindfulness and people are teaching what they call listening. They are teaching these as two separate concepts. Listening as thinking is being taught in universities and colleges. The way they are getting to the work I do is by calling it mindfulness.

This woman was asked if she knew of mindful listening. She responded that yes she did. She knew a bit about yoga and meditation and practiced those modalities. For me that showed that she was so out of touch. She was demonstrating what is being taught in universities.

The concept of Empowered Mindful Listening™ is so new that I don't have to worry about people plagiarizing what I have to say. I'm going to look at where my promise is taking me, and I'm capable.

I'm open to and willing to release any grudges and hostility against academia. They live clearly in their heads and not their bodies and souls. I get it. I haven't always been this compassionate. I've been angry about it. That's my growth.

All of the components of Empowered Mindful Listening™-- holding people as capable, as leaders with respect, and being in cooperation and in partnership-- that's Empowered Mindful Listening™.

That's one of my promises--to intensify what Empowered Mindful Listening™ really is. It's important to demonstrate and be an example of Empowered Mindful Listening™.

We are an example of any of the 5 components of Empowered Mindful Listening™. Am I an example of leadership? Am I an example of partnership? Am I a living example of listening with respect? Am I a living example of partnership and cooperation? In any moment am I a living example of Empowered Mindful Listening™?

As I am having this conversation, I'm having the thought that a homework assignment for future clients is be a living example of one of the components of listening for a year. You are to live one whole year as an example of leadership. Now take that one on, present company included.

I have been constructing a letter to Pharrell Williams in my head. Today I will actually put that down on paper. I want to reach out and ask him to be a sponsor for what I am doing. I have the thought that he would do that. The other person that comes to mind who would do that is Ellen DeGeneres.

Tuck: Do you have a YouTube Channel?

Carol McCall, PhD: Yes, and I have also been asked to do a TEDx Talk. Yes.

Tuck: Do I just keep asking you? Do I hold you accountable?

Carol McCall, PhD: All of the above.

I will take it as my cheerleader supporting me to keep my promise and to break through to the little 3 year old thought form that is scared and believes that if I take my promise on they'll kill me. No they won't.

I promise to have a conversation with my little 3 year old thought form, so that she will feel safe and we can all move forward. That thought form has had a huge impact on me and how far I have come. I will have that conversation with her to allow us all to move forward. I will ask my 3 year old, "What do I need to provide you and what will I promise you?"

That's my promise to you, Tuck.

Tuck: Your work with Werner Erhard has deeply impacted the way you do your work and teach this work. There were a lot of others who studied with him. Where are they, Carol? Or, have you done something different with his work that others have not?

Carol McCall, PhD: He did not add a spiritual component to his work. He stayed with the physical, the intellectual and the emotional.

Tuck: How do you bring the spiritual component into your work?

Carol McCall, PhD: I'm clear that all of this work stems from God. I know Werner believed in God but he never presented it as the nucleus of his work. I'm clear that it is the nucleus of my work. The safest place to present this work is listening, knowing that God is the nucleus. Presenting listening is what people can hear. People know they don't listen.

People can hear the word intuition. They can hear the word gut level. They can hear the word active listening skills. They can hear things that are intellectual for them, and yet I'm clear my message of Empowered Mindful Listening™ is fourfold: mental, physical, emotional and spiritual.

I know the spiritual component of listening because I've had the experience over and over again.

I was giving a workshop for people once who were Seventh-Day Adventists. It was the listening course. It had nothing to do with religion.

One of the participants said, "This work that you are doing is God's work. How come you don't talk about it as God's work?" I answered, because I am not into talking with people about their relationship with God.

However I know that when you really get the level of work that I do, you realize it is God's work. I know I am doing God's work. I know this work is spiritual so I don't have to say it.

47

I don't want to work with people who are righteous and part of the religious right. I don't want to deal with that. I know that God understands that. I present in a format where the masses can hear it. I do know that subliminally they get that this is God's work.

This work is my ministry. I've known that for a long time. I even married a minister. The marriage lasted 18 months. I could not and did not choose to be first lady of the church.

Are you sobbing over there?

Tuck: Uh huh. You have given me a whole new gestalt for listening in the last 10 minutes.

Carol McCall, PhD: Shall we now continue with the 5 sub-categories of Empowered Mindful Listening™- Capability, Leadership, Respect, Partnership and Cooperation?

Empowered Mindful Listening™ is about choosing a way to listen to the world. **However it is that I listen to myself, I will listen to the world that way.**

I've had people say that if you are choosing a particular way of listening then you are not listening. You are always choosing a way to listen. Whether you realize it or not, when you are not listening you're still choosing even though you are not consciously choosing. You are listening from the place of "well, this person is a jerk," or "what do they have to say?" or "they don't know what they are talking about." You have already chosen that way of listening and your listening goes into a filter.

You might as well choose a style of listening that will empower you and the person to whom you are listening to feel safe. However, when you are listening to that person as "I don't believe you," you've already chosen a way to listen. The filter they are speaking into is "I don't believe you." Now shift it to "okay, this person is capable." I don't care what they say I will listen to them as capable. They are capable of anything.

That brings me to how I listen to my son's wife. She is capable of anything. So I still have Empowered Mindful Listening™. You can take it positively or negatively. She is capable of anything. I have experienced that. So does that mean I diminish her? No, I hold her fully capable. Right now my experience of her has not served me. Yet I hold her as capable however she shows up.

Capability

People are capable of being homeless. People are capable of transcendence. People are capable of rising to their highest good and transcending their lower self. That is the beauty of capability. People are capable of rising above their lowest vibration. I find that totally and completely exhilarating and exciting. That is the listening I have with people. I hold them as capable. They are capable of anything.

One of the clients I am coaching right now says to me often, "I don't believe you said that." When someone makes that statement, what they are saying is that they don't hold the speaker as capable. People are capable of anything. Whether they do hold another as capable or not has everything to do with their own structure and their own confidence. However, they are capable of doing anything and everything. We come here fully capable. So my listening is then, "okay, they are capable." They are capable of not being capable, so it's still in that vein.

Leadership

Moving onto leadership, leaders are people who lead themselves in any shape and form. Leadership is about how a person leads himself or herself. How do you lead yourself? What initiatives do you take to move yourself forward? Therein lies the leadership. Leaders can set examples of behavior for people; however, how are they leading themselves? Therein lies the leadership. How do you lead you? Where are you headed in terms of your own leadership style?

Do you initiate? Do you follow through? Do you keep your promises to yourself? Do you honor your own patterns and structures for getting things done? How do you lead you? That's leadership.

Respect

Respect is honoring however people show up. Right now there is a big thing about the Islamic religion. People who practice the Islamic religion are called Muslims. All Muslims are not terrorists, just like all African-Americans are not drug addicts, drug dealers or pimps. Ethnics have had to go through their own rights of passage in terms of stereotypes. All ethnic groups have been stereotyped. All groups have been stereotyped. In terms of being stereotyped it's useful to respect how people have chosen to best express themselves.

When a person has been stereotyped in any form, what possible chance does that person have to be authentic? How do you express who you really are? How do you express your authenticity? How you do that requires respect and honor for yourself. Would I do it that way? No, and that doesn't mean I don't respect you. I respect your right to express yourself. Therein lies the reciprocity. Therefore, I require that you respect my right to express myself. That is the area of respect.

Partnership

The next listening is that of partnership which is my favorite. Partnership means I operate and I take action 100% in this partnership. You take action 100% and you give 100%. This bit about 50/50 is half-assed for me. I'm not interested in half-assed partnership. I'm interested in 100% participation. That's partnership. You give 100% and I give 100%.

Cooperation

Cooperation means, if your methodology or your modality for resolving and having this project come to fruition, if your way of doing it serves the project, then we are going to do it your way. So I "co-operate." I do it in cooperation with you. I do it the way you do it. That's cooperation. It is not "do it my way."

If my way works to the fruition of the project or the event, then you do it the way I do it. That doesn't mean you don't bring your insight and you do it the way I do it. That's cooperation. It's about how does the project get accomplished. How do we blend the way we both do it? If we blend the way we both do it and it works for the good of the project, then we both give our 100% in this particular phase. We may do it 100% your way in this phase and then 100% my way in the next phase. In phase 3 and/or 4 we may blend our ways together to bring the project to fruition. That is switching back and forth among which ways best serve the project

When we talk about Empowered Mindful Listening™ we are listening from one of the 5 substructures and life moves very quickly and flawlessly. It's actually fun. These are the 5 sub-structures of Empowered Mindful Listening™: Listening with leadership, capability, respect, partnership and cooperation. Any input or feedback?

Tuck: I have two questions. One has to do with my remembering or thinking I remember when we were in your 2 workshops, the Advanced Women's Intensive workshop and the Empowered Mindful Listening™ workshop. In one we used all 5 substructures and in the other we only used 3. Is that true and if it is true how come?

Carol McCall, PhD: In the mindful listening work, the Empowered Mindful Listening™ workshop* (see Glossary) was designed to draw men into the course. When men began to show up I narrowed the 5 substructures to 3 which were leadership, capability and respect.

There was a greater male dominated listening style for the 3 categories of leadership, capability and respect. Partnership and cooperation tend to be more female dominated listening styles. Women understand cooperation and partnership. Men talk about cooperation and partnership; however, it has a different vibration to it.

Tuck: Map that onto to how we as women go into cooperation and partnership in relationship with men in terms of listening since listening is vital to a relationship.

Carol McCall, PhD: It's more natural to who we are and to our socialization. Women are socialized to partner. Men are socialized to compete. While they can go into partnership, there is an undercurrent of competition. I'm not saying that women don't go into competition. It looks different though.

Tuck: With where we are today, in terms of the feminine re-emergence and aspects of the feminine coming more into balance with women and men, would you add those last two styles to your workshops with men? There do seem to be more women in what used to be men dominated roles.

Carol McCall, PhD: Don't get seduced that we have more women. Our government is still male dominated. No, we haven't come full circle yet where women are on a level playing field in terms of feminine energy. The feminine energy is coming more to the forefront; however, it is still a male dominated world.

To answer your question, would I now include the 5 categories in the Empowered Mindful Listening™* workshop? As an inform I intend to do the Empowered Mindful Listening™ workshop online. My intention is to get feedback from my audience as to whether or not to include partnership and cooperation. I trust that the energy will tell me whether or not to include it. I'm not about being right but informed and updated.

Even if this is the 21st Century it is still a male dominated culture that I live in. Has the male energy included more of its own femininity into its own psyche? I don't know. I've seen information about men staying at home, raising the children and being real fathers. I don't know. I know what I see. I don't always believe what I see in terms of media. I want to see for myself. I have confidence that I will get that from the audience.

Tuck: My other question had to do with capability and how this tool of Empowered Mindful Listening™ with capability is a way out of codependency?

Carol McCall, PhD: Absolutely it is a way out. I'm coaching a man now who has been in a relationship with a woman for 13 years. She has been "clamoring" (his words) to get married. He is resistant to getting married and he has been up front about it. He doesn't want to make this kind of commitment. For him, being in relationship with her has been a long commitment. That's a long commitment for him. In terms of codependency he has counted on her to ignore her needs because he has not held her as capable.

He refers to himself as having been in this directorial role with her. I shared with him that he does not hold her as capable. He shared that she responds well when he directs her. I said then that is how come she has periods where (in his words) she goes off the deep end. She is breaking out of your super imposed limitations that you have placed on her called, "she is not capable." I think she is highly capable, but not if you are in the directorial role. People who are capable don't need a director. For 13 years he has been directing her.

When you hold people as capable it crushes codependency. It also means that the person who holds others as capable also has to be unattached.

Tuck: I actually remember you coaching someone around his or her family at one of your workshops. It was challenging for you to get them to see that the person in their family was highly capable, even capable of being "a victim." It was subtle but a very rich interaction. You described the individual as being capable of doing anything and everything. This tool really does pull people out of victimhood and that's huge.

Carol McCall, PhD: If people choose to be in victimhood, they are capable of doing that. Leave them alone.

Tuck: Sounds so simple!

Carol McCall, PhD: In its simplicity comes the strength to keep practicing unattachment. People want to go in and help. It's very seductive.

Tuck: I want you to speak something you've shared with me before that completely changed my perception. You are the only one I've heard share this distinction. Share the difference please between being detached, unattached and attached.

Carol McCall, PhD: Attached is the backside of the hand. Detached is the front side of the hand. Unattached is neutral. When someone is attached it is what it means. You are attached to it. It is like Velcro. You are stuck to it. There is a lot of energy on it. However, unlike Velcro, people have to keep applying the energy. At least with Velcro all you have to do is stick it on and it stays. With attachment you have to keep rethinking and rethinking in order to stay there to keep it glued. You keep bringing it back which keeps you attached.

Detached is you keep having to remind yourself, "I'm not going to think about it, I'm not going to think about it," while you are thinking about it. It's "don't think about it" while you are thinking about it. I'm not going to think about it. I'm going to put it on the top shelf, except that you remember you put it on the top shelf.

Unattached is that you are neutral. It doesn't matter. There is no energy. I use the example of looking at the walls in your house. Do you walk into your house saying, "Look at these walls. I have to do something about these walls. These walls are really upsetting me." No, you walk into your house and see the color of your walls and are totally neutral. You are totally neutral. The only attachment you might have could be that the walls are bare in which case you can get something to put on the walls. However you are neutral about the colors. If you are not, you change them so you can become neutral. That is what unattached is. You are neutral.

Tuck: In the lesson of learning to feel into my own energy and that of others, that is one of the greatest exercises I have ever been able to practice. Am I attached when I speak or when others are speaking to me? Sometimes when I hear people tell me they are unattached and that they are over something, I energetically feel detachment. I don't feel that they are unattached or neutral. Those 3 distinctions have been huge for me.

Carol McCall, PhD: Yes, they are very powerful.

What is the goal? Men ask this one a lot. I'm not anti-male. I am enthusiastically entertained by the male psyche. What is the goal? The goal is to be neutral.

Tuck: Is it in listening they ask that question or in everything they ask that question?

Carol McCall, PhD: In everything. When you really consider listening, what are we doing all the time, Tuck? We are listening. The minute we developed little ears in utero at 21 weeks, we have the ability to listen and to hear. That's when we started listening. How does a child learn to speak? By listening. What are you doing with all the noise in your head? You are listening. I don't care what words people use for it. You are listening to your thoughts. You are always, always, always listening.

Bringing it down to that simplicity, I don't care what people call it. You are still listening. Who are you listening to? **The goal is to be neutral, neutral in your listening.**

Tuck: That's an intriguing exercise, not just in our interaction or in interacting with others, but particularly with myself and God. To stop the chatter is a challenge. To be unattached and find that place of neutrality can be a challenge. That is still taking practice.

Carol McCall, PhD: Absolutely. As many years as I have been doing this work, and you know that has been many years, the majority of my life, I still practice neutrality. One of the things my daughter marvels at is how quiet it is around me. That's because I practice that kind of neutrality so that it is quiet. It's got to be quiet.

Tuck: Right now I feel a new sense of listening, reverence and knowing. There is an empowerment that is available empathically when I listen to myself from a place of being unattached. It is quiet.

Perhaps there is nothing to listen to but the divine. I'm not articulating this well, and perhaps that's because there is nothing to articulate. There is power in listening to myself as nothing. How can I do that with you if I am not doing it with myself, and with leadership, capability, respect, partnership and cooperation? I like this tool!!

Carol McCall, PhD: Here is the good news. You, as your higher self, you don't have to practice anything. You already are those tools. What you are doing is bringing them forth in terms of recognizing you already are that. There is nothing to practice in your higher self.

Tuck: There is a surge of love in my heart. I get it.

Carol McCall, PhD: Nothing to practice. It's who you already are.

Tuck: Dr. C that is rich. It feels so pure.

Carol McCall, PhD: When you practice from this level you are accessing what you already are and who you already are.

Tuck: Thank you.

Carol McCall, PhD: You are welcome.

#4

BEING HEARD

A SPEAKING AND LISTENING STYLE THAT ALLOWS BOTH SPEAKER AND LISTENER TO EXPERIENCE A COMPLETE EXCHANGE IN THE COURSE OF CONVERSATION.

Carol McCall, PhD: The next tool is Being Heard. I had a thought the other day in terms of this tool and you communicating with people in your women's group. I wonder if you experience Being Heard. Do you experience Being Heard in your women's group? If not, then how come? So that's my first question, do you experience Being Heard in your women's group?

Tuck: Sometimes yes and sometimes no. Some individuals absolutely hear me and some individuals do not, so it is a yes and a no.

Carol McCall, PhD: Okay that makes sense.

Tuck: I don't feel heard by the group overall.

Carol McCall, PhD: Okay? What is the ultimate goal for your group in Being Heard?

Tuck: The first word that comes to me is understanding and then acceptance.

I am practicing understanding and acceptance for myself and others in the group. My intention is to be clear and bold in my communication and not go into doubt, criticism and judgment of myself in hindsight. I "make up" that being clear and bold in my communication sometimes comes across as being a bully. So acceptance and understanding of me is a goal.

It is also a goal and practice for me to accept others where they are, and at the same time, be courageous enough to give bold authentic feedback as to how I experience their participation in the group. My commitment is to practice mindful/empowered listening with each woman and hold her as capable, hold her as a leader and hold her with respect.

Being in a group and community of women presents me with an incredible opportunity to use The Nine Tools of Empowered Mindful Listening™, because it is about communication and relationships, individually and collectively. I'm a work in progress and, again, it's an incredible opportunity to practice The Nine Tools of Empowered Mindful Listening™.

Carol McCall, PhD: Two women in your circle know my work. I know you are certainly Being Heard, understood, and accepted by these two women.

The other part is about agreement. We can stand side by side and not agree. I accept your perspective as yours. The key word here is acceptance. You have a right to have your perspective about it and mine is different.

What many people think about agreement/acceptance is that if I accept what you say I have to agree or I have to think the way you think. That's not it at all. So Being Heard has those

3 components, "The 3 A's" of Acceptance, Appreciation and Acknowledgment.

Listening without having to agree is a very vital piece about Being Heard. It's one of the reasons I say that people don't listen. When they listen they have a mischievous thought that says, "When I listen, and I get your perspective, then I have to change my perspective." However, that is not accurate. You don't have to change your perspective.

I can have clarity about your perspective and not share your perspective. **Being Heard means you have experienced that rare trilogy of being accepted, appreciated and acknowledged.**

People don't have to agree with you. They can still accept, appreciate and acknowledge you. That's rare. You are smart enough to have formed a community that allows that to happen for you.

When I first started doing this work many years ago, I kept looking outside of myself, to society, to my family, to my community, to friends, to the church, for like- minded people. They didn't exist in the places I was looking. The closest I came was when I was on staff with Werner Erhard and was trained by him. That's the closest I came. Then I really didn't come close until I formed my own company with Thomas Leonard.

Thomas and I formed the College of Life Planning back in 1988 together. Interestingly enough I was leaving Werner's staff when Thomas was fired from his staff. Werner fired him. Very few people know that. Thomas was a genius. He was truly a genius. I think his IQ was around 180 or something like that.

Thomas said, "28 to 30 years from now coaching will be one of the primary ways of people being served and supported." He said, "Carol, they won't even know your name. They won't even know who you are." That was a terrible blow to my ego since I was on the forefront of coaching. We were taking a lot of the modeling from Werner's coaching and training. He trained his trainers in a model very similar to the one I use to train our coaches.

It's a very succinct and simple model because it can be duplicated and followed, and it's very rigorous. It gets in people's faces, which is exactly what it is supposed to do.

If you are going to be a coach, you really do need to have your own "crap" handled so that you don't unknowingly and even mischievously blend in with other people's patterns. We each individually have enough of our own patterns that we don't want to comingle it with others.

Being Heard is a tool that can separate your patterns from someone else's and make sure that you are heard. I don't have to agree, and I'm clear that I heard you.

My daughter and I share that a lot. We share that separation of our patterns. Last night she came to get herself cleared (meaning, communicating out loud so that she hears her thoughts, slowing down her thoughts so that the she can have clarity about what she is thinking). That's the word she and I use. She came to get cleared. We get cleared as we are Being Heard.

So Being Heard is that tool where you have to have the 3 A's, Acknowledgment, Acceptance and Appreciation. Acknowledgment doesn't necessarily mean I agree. Acceptance doesn't have to mean I agree. Appreciation doesn't mean agreement. It simply means, "I get it." I am present to the full communication without Criticism, Condemnation and Judgment. That's it.

I know I lose interest with people who don't finish their sentences. They will say,

"You know." "We went down, you know..." "We went to the movies, you know." No, I don't know.

I'm so committed to communication. There are times when I am required to finish my own thoughts. I am working to finish my own communication to be complete. The way that happens for me is when I slow down. Then I can speak confidently. I can speak with certainty about the words I choose to deliver my message.

I have a commitment to Being Heard. **It's my responsibility to be heard. It is not your responsibility to make sure I am heard. It is my responsibility as the speaker to make sure my message is received the way I intended it to be received. It's your responsibility to listen and to respect the message.**

Whether you agree or not, it is your responsibility to make sure that you heard what the message is. When you do that you are in communication. You are in communication and in communion. You are in union with you and with me. I trust the tool of Being Heard.

Very few people know the power of Being Heard. When I experienced Being Heard the first time, which was by Werner, I sobbed. Literally, I sobbed. After that, I experienced Being Heard by Virginia Satir. Actually I experienced the way she listened. I experienced the way people were heard by her. It was from that experience that I chose to listen to people like Virginia did. I had the thought that I'm going to listen like she did. So I had a role model in terms of listening. She profoundly impacted me.

Then getting trained by Werner in terms of listening, and joining his consulting group, also impacted me. That is exactly what we did, we in consulting services. We were trained in consulting services to listen, very similarly to how I learned to listen with Virginia Satir.

All that training came together for me and I began and developed my work. And, I developed my own community. It was the only place where like-minded people came. They came to my work. It became my community.

I think it is smart for people to form their own community. It is different from cliques. I find cliques have no respect for one another. There is the "covert agreement" to think, feel and act the same way, to stay in their "comfort" zone. They have "covertly" agreed not to feel differently, not to change or not to grow.

Tuck: Cliques bore me. I don't like them.

I want to go back to a previous conversation. This may not be so much about the tool as it is Thomas Leonard's comment that no one would remember you. How does that comment feel to you today?

Carol McCall, PhD: At the time it felt personal. Today it is spot on. It was accurate. The ego with me still resents not being recognized for being one of the early pioneers of coaching. My ego feels dishonored. However, when I have allowed my ego to rule that situation I see the futility of it.

There are very few people in the International Coaching Federation, which Thomas Leonard founded, and very few long timers, who still know who I am. There are very few and they are dying out quickly. The ego says, "You are supposed to know who I am. You are supposed to come find me. I'm one of the pioneers. I have to meet your requirements?"

The ego goes through all of that and you know what? They really don't care. It's like the weather. The weather really doesn't care.

Either make your contribution or continue doing what you are doing or not, **and**, get over it.

I'm coming up on renewal time for my Master Certification as a Coach. The ego says, "I shouldn't have to renew. I'm one of the founders." However, those are the rules, so renew. Okay so I'm pulling my paperwork together so I can renew. I have to have my courses approved by them. The ego would say, "Renew my coaching courses? Are you kidding? The foundation of your coaching is mine. I'm supposed to be approved?"

Tuck: I once heard the quote, "A person with an experience is never at the mercy of a person with a theory." So you can talk theory to me all day long. You can talk the theory of listening to me all day long. It's like you said on the Listening Panel that day, **"Talking about listening is an oxymoron."**

My commitment in 2018 and going forward is to have very bold conversations with myself and others.

I happened to Google Werner while we are talking. I don't know him from Adam's house cat, nor do I know whether he is dead or living.

Carol McCall, PhD: He's alive.

Tuck: He's alive? So I googled Werner and Thomas Leonard and I see a legacy, a long list of names, and your name is not there. I am shocked.

What is it you and I desire and expect from the Universe so that people have the opportunity to fully experience this work of Empowered Mindful Listening™?

This Listening work is inclusive. The paradigms of duality are so obvious to me today. Listening and presence is inclusive and applicable to everything- relationships, work, finances, and health, all of life.

I am exuberant when individuals have the opportunity to experience your work and your listening. I know the results. I've experienced them personally and through others. I know how your work transforms people. I have experienced the difference in my husband, daughter, siblings, colleagues and friends. It's a visceral and energetic feeling for me.

Maybe, Dr. C, this is the way people feel after they talk to me. (Laughing).

I so clearly see and feel the results in people's life and in their communication when they coach with you. It is powerful. It IS powerful for people to be heard. I am feeling the results of Being Heard myself. It's powerful.

And, it's challenging work. My friend calls after her coaching session with you and tells me she's exhausted. Working on us is challenging. Listening to others and to ourselves takes work. And, it's empowering.

Do you believe people are attracted to this work because they are ready?

How do we attract people who have their heads down working hard and don't stop long enough to listen to the gift of Being Heard?

Carol McCall, PhD: What that brought up for me was the story Buckminster Fuller told long ago. He said there are 4 kinds of people. Those of us who call ourselves awakened and enlightened run around trying to wake up 3 of the 4 kinds of people

We'll go to the first group of people. They are sound asleep. We shake them and try to wake them up. We get excited and enthusiastic. The best they can do is stir. If anything, they give us the raspberry and we get our feelings hurt.

The best thing we can do is to straighten the covers, fluff up the pillow, kiss them on the forehead and move to the next group.

The second group is already stirring. They are in a drowsy kind of sleep. We go, "Oh good! They are about to wake up. Let me go wake them up." We go shake them. We try to wake them. They give us the raspberry, and we get our feelings hurt.

Again, we straighten up the covers. We fluff the pillow, kiss them on the forehead, and move on.

The third group is sitting up and their eyes are open. However, this is as far as they are going to go. They are just sitting up. They are not going to get up. They are not going any further than where they are.

Our job is again to straighten the covers, fluff the pillow and kiss them on the forehead and move to the fourth group.

The last group is standing up and they say to you, "It's about time you got here!"

These are the ones you align yourself with and create a vortex, an energy field that will draw groups one, two and three to group four. You become a magnet. You attract them by your energy and by your modeling and consistency.

"Leave them alone. They will come home" (according to Little Bo Peep) drawn by the energy that has been created.

If you want to be heard, align yourself with the group that is already putting out the message, consistently, consistently and consistently.

Isn't that a great story?

Tuck: Yes, I am taking notes. I have the 14th Gene Key* of Bounteousness in my Attractor Field of the Golden Pathway*. The essence of my energy in that Gene Key is the Shadow of Compromise, the Gift expression of Competency and the highest expression, which is the Siddhi of Bounteousness. Bounteousness carries with it enthusiasm, flair, flexibility and efficiency. (*Refer to the Glossary for information about the Gene Keys and The Golden Pathway.)

So I am listening to you because I realize that I probably spend a lot of time screaming in the ears of groups one, two and three, like it is going to make a difference. It's as if I am "doing" Bounteousness as opposed to "being" Bounteousness.

Acceptance, appreciation and acknowledgment take me back to my conversations from earlier this week.

I experienced acceptance. It also felt like appreciation. The words I kept hearing in my head from my work with you were, "You are gathering information, Tuck. This is good. You are gathering information about who the other person is, where they are and how they think and feel."

I practiced the tool of acknowledgement as well by saying, "I hear you." However, we look at the guidelines for our community differently; we are going to have to agree that we disagree.

My question around these three components of Being Heard, Acceptance, Acknowledgment and Appreciation, relates to a particular situation with a group. If the group has a set of guidelines each person has agreed to, is it possible to have a situation where we can agree to disagree? How do we navigate a situation of disagreement if there are rules and guidelines that must be adhered to in order to participate in the group?

Carol McCall, PhD: That's a time bomb. It's a lie. If you don't agree, you are not going to agree to disagree. You can't attempt to fit yourself into an agreement in which you don't agree. That's a time bomb. It's a lie.

Tuck: What if the other person sees the guidelines as just that, guidelines? If the guidelines are the structure, what do you do?

Let's look at your listening work. It's a structure for listening. If I come into your coaching community and make a commitment to align myself with your listening tools, and then later come along and say, "Well Dr. C, they are just tools. I don't know if I agree with them."

Am I compromising your community if I'm no longer in alignment with your tools?

What would happen if I viewed them as mutable, malleable and changeable based on time, evolution and personality? How does that feel to you?

Carol McCall, PhD: I invite people to leave. I openly invite people to leave. I've had that experience. I've even had people come into the community and argue with me about the tools. They disagree with the concept of the tools. But, they haven't practiced them. They haven't lived them.

If you haven't practiced the tools or lived them and still continue to disagree, then leave and start your own system.

Tuck: Practice them and live them.

Carol McCall, PhD: Until you have practiced and lived my tools, you don't have a basis on which to disagree with them.

My tools are an amalgamation of much of the work I've done since 1960. I've worked with great thought-leaders. I've taken concepts here and concepts there and pulled them together for myself.

I didn't agree with everything Buckminster Fuller said. I didn't agree with everything Werner said. I didn't agree with everything Virginia Satir said. I didn't agree with everything Gestalt Theory talked about. I didn't agree with all of the family systems information.

I took the richness of each source and then I simplified them. My gift is to make things simple. I am a Master at simplifying some of the most complicated concepts.

When information gets too complicated I leave. I'm clear life was not designed to be complicated. Life was designed to be simple. I didn't say easy. I said simple. **Life is very simple. Our opinions, thoughts and analysis are what complicate life.**

One of the reasons Psychology doesn't have a primary status is that it has false clout. It has a type of false power. It doesn't stand up in court. It doesn't create any laws that we live by. It has a false kind of position in our culture. Psychology was developed by the ego. The ego has formed an entire industry about and around itself.

Tuck: That's so funny!!

Carol McCall, PhD: Psychology has intimidated people for years from the ego.

Freud was afraid of women. He didn't understand the menstrual cycle. He didn't understand hormonal balance, none of it. So he ended up saying it was the women who had all of the sexual problems. He projected all of his inhibitions onto women because he did not understand them.

At that time and still, men do rule the laws and the structures of our society. They make them. Look at Congress. So yes, who is abolishing the family and places where you can get abortions? It's not the women.

I'm on Thomas's site right now and it says, "The father of coaching." He and I started training in 1988. That's when we started together in San Francisco.

It wasn't a lie that he said no one will know who you are. The reason he said that is because, Tuck, and I don't say this often, I have not wanted to be responsible for that many people. I haven't. I like controlling my community. (The ego likes the thought of controlling its community.)

Have I gotten past that? Yes. I absolutely have and I see the disservice that my ego has provided for me. I don't have to be responsible for billions and billions of people. I only have to be responsible for the message. How arrogant of me to think that it, the ego, had to be responsible for 8 billion people.

No, "it", the ego, simply has to be responsible for the message.

I am not responsible for delivering the message to everyone. So in 2018 I am in complete alignment with getting the message out to those who are standing up, ready to move forward. They will hear the message and they will come.

People still come to my site with the minimal amount of marketing that I do. People still say, "I want to know more about what you do." That's a result of the internet, which I boycotted for two years. I did not deliver the message. So am I over that? As of today I am, yes.

Am I over it, meaning am I over feeling responsible for everyone? Yes, and this is the first time I have listened to myself make this distinction. I have been remiss in getting the message out. Thank you, Tuck. I have been heard by you. It's about the message, not about the people. They will come. The message needs to get out there. I am committed to getting it out in 2018 and for the rest of my life.

Tuck: I am having the thought about saying to people, "You are not listening." Can I say that?

Carol McCall, PhD: It's said all the time. "You are not listening." What are our children yelling to their parents? "You are not listening." Absolutely you can say that with full credibility. It's the truth.

Tuck: My follow up statement to "You are not listening" is not meant to be a derogatory or judgmental comment. It is, "I know you are not listening because you don't know how." We don't know what we don't know. That's how it feels to me.

I know when people are listening or not. I know it. I can feel it.

So are you going to do your TEDx Talk this year?

Carol McCall, PhD: I'm not making that commitment yet.

Tuck: What would be the most comfortable for you? Thomas Leonard and others created industries out of egotistic means of communicating.

If the form and activity didn't matter, and you had the chance to share your work like what we are doing now, what would that be?

What I see for you is to have someone ask you questions, where you could respond, perhaps on video. It doesn't have to be a TEDx environment. It's more about where can someone get you on video. We are doing this audio, which is good. I can see something going viral that's really powerful.

The most powerful statement you've made to me over the last 6 months about listening was the question you asked on the panel. The question was, "How do you **talk** about listening?" I've repeated it and shared it with others. They are stunned and then they say, "You are absolutely correct."

Carol McCall, PhD: Right. It's an oxymoron. How do you talk about listening? You don't. You **practice** listening. Keep your mouth closed and you listen. You practice and practice. I really get it.

Right now, I am so thrilled with this conversation today. I have made a valuable distinction between the message and being responsible for the people and the last remnants of fear have left me. I knew that I was fearful of something from my early childhood as well as some recent experiences. As I face those experiences I am able to face anything.

Today what I was fearful of has been identified. I only have to deliver the message. I don't have to take care of everyone and whether they get it or not.

I can be responsible to thousands of people by delivering the message. **Listening is the message.** I'm the messenger and I lost touch with that truth. The ego really distorted that for me. I get it. Thank you, Tuck. I had no idea what Being Heard was going to evolve into today. I knew we would talk about the tool of Being Heard and the components of it. Those components are rich.

Tuck: In our conversation last week, there was a moment in Being Heard where you were explaining to me what it was like for you to be heard. You said, "It was like being listened to by God." We were both in tears.

There is clarity for me in these conversations with you when there is nothing in the space, when the vacuum is there. When the space is open, when I am listening and Being Heard, the ego is not operating and trying to direct the conversation. This isn't about what I can say or what you can say. We are both completely open to the results of the work, that of Being Heard and The Nine Tools of Empowered Mindful Listening™.

It is amazing how God shows up. That's how I feel this conversation is. There is an opening for Source Intelligence and God. It's fascinating. Look at God beneath your wings right now. The empowerment of the God force that shows up is amazing.

I pulled out your Human Energy Design* (see Glossary) chart as I was listening to you as you spoke about what was being transformed and what opened up for you. I look at the deep imprinting of Purpose in your chart that reveals the service you are here to be in the world.

Your voice in the world is to empower clarity. Your Purpose and passion is around clarity and intuition. Your way of navigating communication with yourself, others and God is in a complete state of freedom, in a partnership that's deep.

That partnership feels like what you and I experience. The talent you bring to the table is this uncanny ability to speak the words of truth, where there is this essence of integrity and impeccability in the flow and the structure of your words. Again, it is in the truth of the words and the impeccability of your words. That's your talent.

Your ultimate contribution in the world is that of a complete rebirth of language. Look at what you are doing with the little thing that people call listening. People talk about passive and active listening. We are

flippant about the word listening when actually there is so much juice and rebirth in The Nine Tools of Empowered Mindful Listening™. OMG!

Is this how we all get to the heart of creation? Through listening? I'm having such a good time listening to myself. (Laughing) It's time to deliver the message.

Carol McCall, PhD: Today was a renewal of the first time I "listened to" myself say what has kept me in a certain status and place in terms of delivering the message. It was a distortion. I had to be responsible for the people.

No, I don't have to be responsible for the people. I only am "required" to be responsible for delivering the message. That's what I signed on for, to deliver the message.

Tuck: In Human Design language you are a 4th line. This line carries a missionary quality. People with a 4th line have a message to deliver to the world. This person can never change the message. She can change the people to whom she delivers the message. She can never change the message.

Carol McCall, PhD: I signed up to deliver the message. The message is listening. I'm near tears I'm so excited.

Tuck: That makes me happy. I'm a believer that my energy of enthusiasm, flair, flexibility and efficiency is what will attract people to this beautiful field of energy you are creating.

Carol McCall, PhD: Simply deliver the message. I am liberated. I am so proud and pleased to intuitively know and have our partnership at this stage of our lives. **This is our time.** You have asked, "How come you are doing this?" **I am compelled to do no other.** When I move from this place, I don't question it.

Thank you. I experienced Being Heard.

#5

BOLDNESS

A SPEAKING STYLE THAT IS "TRUE" TO THE MOMENT, EVENT, CIRCUMSTANCE.

Tuck: In The Human Energy Design System* (see Glossary), we share the belief that as a human species we are evolving from "thinking" human beings to "solar plexus" beings. I interpret that to mean that we are raising our individual awareness and frequencies and, ultimately, the chemistry of who we are, so that we aren't hooked by our reactive behaviors and emotional responses. From my perspective, living as a "solar plexus" being is being present and listening mindfully.

How I respond to life has everything to do with attitude. Attitude has everything to do with presence and how I interpret my environment. It is how I perceive what is happening to me in the moment and, most importantly, how I respond. As I hold a thought, every thought has a chemical and emotional component, which is translated chemically in my body and physiology. This is how I create my reality. If my intention is to raise my awareness and frequency, then it would serve for me to be present and to practice listening mindfully, yes?

I was in a workshop last week with a good friend of mine. She is an Intuitive and teaches intuition. She spoke about how when working with clients around their intuition she listens to them. By that she meant to "not make gestures" in response to what her clients are saying but to go into that space where she is silent. She is not analyzing what the client is saying. She is not thinking about her response. She is allowing the client to be where they are with what they are speaking, without interjecting. I got so excited. She was describing your work and style of mindful listening.

She was describing the space of listening, the field, space and dimension where we are all connected. I love it when you share the statement, "No two things can occupy the same space at the same time." To me, this is listening mindfully. This is listening as love. This is empathy. This is the place where we are connected and at one.

People today talk a lot about raising awareness and how to do that, and connecting to their higher selves. We use the words empathic and intuition like they are something special and unique. We are all empathic and intuitive. The Nine Tools of Empowered Mindful Listening™ are powerful in providing practices for the skills of listening, intuition and empathy.

So go ahead and talk to me about Boldness. (Laughing) I'm intriguing myself today with my thinking and am apparently quite full of myself.

Carol McCall, PhD: The way that I'm supporting people to use the tool of Boldness, is to say what is there in the moment. You can only be bold in the moment. It requires people to be fully present to be bold. One of the reasons people are not bold is because they are not present. When you are present and say what is exactly there for you in the moment, something as simple as, "I don't have that answer," or "I have other thoughts right now," that's bold.

Bold doesn't mean confrontational. Being bold means that you are in the present moment and speaking what is there. That's bold. It is also saying something that is blatantly the truth, something that is obvious. What I mean by obvious is that it is reality. It is right here. It is present. Whatever is there in the moment is very clear and to speak that is being bold.

For example, if there is a silence in the room that is deafening, to say, "Goodness it is really quiet in here. I can hear you folks thinking and not speaking." That's bold. It's not confrontational. It's stating what is here in the moment.

It doesn't require confrontation. I have the thought that many people confuse and collapse the distinction between being bold and being rude. Being bold doesn't mean being rude. Being bold means being present and speaking what is there in the moment. I have individuals who ask, "What if what I am thinking isn't appropriate to say?" That's what you say in the moment. "What I am thinking right now isn't appropriate to say." That's bold. "If I said what I was thinking right now, it would not serve the purpose of this conversation." That is a bold statement. However, to blurt out, "You are a jackass and I don't like what you are saying," while that's bold, it is also rude. If your intent is to be rude, then be rude. Simply recognize that is your intent.

Tuck: What was the statement again? "If I said what I was thinking it would not serve." Is that what you said?

Carol McCall, PhD: Yes, if I said what I was thinking right now it would not serve the purpose of our communication.

Tuck: I get the rudeness part. When I think about being bold, what comes up for me is fear. What am I afraid to say? Perhaps I'm making up that there will be confrontation if I speak what's so in the moment. Or, if I speak up in the moment I'm going to be confronted. The word fear comes up immediately. I'm afraid to be bold because I'm afraid of confrontation. What's that about?

Carol McCall, PhD: You've addressed it. You've answered it. You are afraid to be bold, since as far as you are concerned you are going to create a confrontation. You are going to be challenged or you are going to get a confrontation that you can't handle.

Tuck: Uh huh.

Carol McCall, PhD: As far as I can tell there are not any communications that you can't handle. There are communications that you can prefer not to hear. So far, in a civil communication, and by civil I mean those individuals who consider themselves civil, there are no communications that you can't handle. You'll make it through. I'm not talking about "communication bullies." If you are not clear about the purpose of the communication, you ask. That's bold. Is your intent to upset me? Is your intent to disrespect me? Is your intent to diminish me? Is that your intent? Is your intent to embarrass me? That's bold. What's the person's intent?

Rarely will they respond to your question. You are embodying Boldness by asking that question. If someone says, "I didn't dishonor you", I say, **"I didn't say you dishonored me. I said I feel dishonored by how you said what you said. Is that your intent?** The way you said what you said, I feel dishonored. Was that your intent?"

The person then has to wake up to how they are communicating with me.

Tuck: What if the other person says, "You need to work on yourself. Quit projecting onto me. I can't make you feel any way." How would you respond to that?

Carol McCall, PhD: "The way you delivered your message to me, I feel disrespected in the way you delivered your message." If the person says, "You need to work on yourself," then you respond, "I am, by delivering the message I simply delivered about the way you are communicating with me. I am working on myself by sharing with you in this moment the way I feel in how you delivered your message to me."

Tuck: Can I carry you around in my ear? (Laughing) I remember now what the word was that I was trying to grasp in an earlier conversation. This morning I read the 59th Gene Key in *Gene Keys: Unlocking the Higher Purpose Hidden in Your DNA* by Richard Rudd. The Shadow expression of this Gene Key is Dishonesty, the Gift expression is Intimacy and the Highest Expression is Transparency. When I read the meaning of Transparency, the author described your communication and work around listening. It was not what most people think that Intimacy and Transparency describe which is sexual intimacy and connection. Empowered Mindful Listening™ is presence to one's self and another. That is true intimacy and transparency.

This particular Gene Key has to do with breaking through the fear of intimacy and the honesty and transparency required to do that. I'm curious as to what Empowered Mindful Listening™ has to do with fear, from your perspective. Our task in life is to overcome and/or transcend our fears. How does listening relate? When present, there is no fear, right?

Carol McCall, PhD: Correct. No two things can occupy the same space at the same time. So when I'm in fear, I'm not listening. Now, when I pretend that I am listening and I am fearful, I'm not listening to what you are saying. I'm listening to what I think might happen. What if they do this? What if they say something I don't want to hear?

What if, what if, what if? I'm already listening to what if. I'm not listening to you.

Tuck: I catch myself doing that at times. When I do, I can feel I'm not in my body. It's as if I have my hands up and out in front of me trying to control everything and/or protect myself.

Carol McCall, PhD: You can only listen in being. Listening takes place in being. Hearing takes place in the ego. It tries to pretend it is listening. It's an imposter. There are people who pride themselves on listening and being able to repeat word for word what someone says. However, did they get all 4 quadrants - mental, physical, emotional and spiritual? Did they get the full gestalt of my expression? If they did then they are really listening, and there isn't any arrogance.

What you are speaking of is that when you are listening you are in being. People who are terribly afraid of the connection of being are not likely to allow themselves to surrender to that degree. They have mastered **the act and the façade of listening.**

They are listening through a well-defined filter of "you are weak so you need to be dominated." Whatever that filter is determines how they behave. It appears that they are listening; however, they are not. They are hearing.

Most individuals that have mastered the façade of listening have also mastered recognizing patterns. We all have patterns.

When you are quiet and listening, you get a person's patterns very quickly. They tell you in their language. I listen to people's patterns through their language. What language do they use?

This morning I was coaching a client. During our time he used the words, kind of, mostly, and sort of consistently. I asked him if he was aware that he was having me diminish the validity of what he was saying by using those words and not take him seriously.

I kind of do this, and sort of do this and mostly do that. Well, what is it? Do you do it or don't you do it? Saying that to him in that moment was bold, and I was paying attention to what he was saying in the moment. I recognize when people are not bold by the language they use.

Tuck: You did that to me one time.

Carol McCall, PhD: Only once? (Laughing)

Tuck: What I remember was you talking about my inflection. I almost always ask a question, rather than making a statement. I go up at the end of my sentences as if I am asking permission for something, rather than making a statement.

Carol McCall, PhD: By the way, and I am acknowledging you, you rarely do that now in my presence. You make your statements. I have the thought Tuck that you and I don't need the permission. We are completely relaxed in our conversations. There is no need for anything other than our authenticity. That is my experience.

Tuck: I was going to share how safe I feel in conversation with you.

In your listening, and I don't know if you can tie this back to Boldness, how do you determine the Life Decision for people? You have shared you listen to their patterns of communication. Their communication patterns reveal the Life Decision. Is that true?

Carol McCall, PhD: No, after all these years, I get the Life Decision intuitively.

I know the Life Decision so well that when I'm listening to people's words it simply validates what I have already gotten. If I'm not clear I listen.

There is a fine distinction between Not Good Enough/Better Than and Not Enough/Too Much. The distinction is for the Not Good Enough/Better Than; it has to be perfect and correct. That Life Decision consistently has to add something. I don't care what it is.

I had the opportunity to share with someone who has that Life Decision. I had an idea I preferred, and I was careful to use that language. I said, "I have an idea that I prefer." There was no competition. That was my preference. However, the person with that Life Decision went, "Oh, is your idea better than mine?" I didn't say that. I said this is the one I prefer. I refused to be seduced by the Life Decision that was operating in them at the time.

The Life Decision with me is Not Enough/Too Much. This Life Decision has to do with quantity, not accuracy. The more you give, the more that's there. That's juicy and delicious to me. Does it have to be accurate? I would prefer that it be, however, simply give me a lot. I'll sort it out.

Tuck: So, I'm just curious. Can you intuit the Life Decision for Ellie?

Carol McCall, PhD: Yes, Ellie's Life Decision is Not Good Enough/Better Than. She has to be right about things. There is rigidness about her. She lives in her head. She counts on the rightness of how she sees things. She needs the rigidity and the accurateness. She fills herself with information for validation. She also has a husband who is a psychotherapist, right? She is Not Good Enough to have earned the right to be with this type of person. She is constantly making herself Better Than to live up to what she has already decided she is Not Good Enough about. That's what I got.

Tuck: I am fascinated by the Life Decision. I don't intuit it yet. Last night our women's group had our last call. She literally was not able to access the call to be there on time. We had to begin without her. Once she made it to the call, she was asked to speak and share. She shared she would rather wait to speak as the last person. However, she was dropped off of the call before having time to share and was not present for the end of our final call.

I was playing around in the Not Important/Most Important/ Omnipotent category. That's what came up for me first based on that experience. Then I went to my experience of her rigidity. The Not Important/Most Important/Omnipotent generally does not have that kind of rigidity. She is pretty rigid.

I totally get the rigidity. That's my Not Good Enough/Better Than speaking here. I get that.

Carol McCall, PhD: Yes, with that Life Decision there is a righteousness to being right. It's entrenched in the need to be right. Her request to be part of the brain wave experiment feels more as if she wanted to be "in" on something. It was coming more from being able to be part of the Brain Wave research so that she could be right in her rigidity. I did have that thought of Not Important initially and then I had the thought that the rigidity is the deciding factor.

The Life Decisions are unending in terms of getting into a depth with people. They are right on as well. They permeate through everything. You get it in their language.

Tuck: When you did your first book with John Fogg did you have the tool of Boldness then?

Carol McCall, PhD: Yes.

Tuck: You also had the tool of Silence. I remember that being different. What happened to Silence?

Carol McCall, PhD: I don't have an answer right now. Through the course of the workshops it seemed not as impactful. It didn't stay with people as long as the others did. I get my feedback from my workshops, so in this case I let Silence go. I fine-tune the workshops by my participants and what they are telling me.

Tuck: In The Listening Course (TLC) we had the Trust/Bold exercise, would you still put that one in the course and, if so, what is the purpose?

Carol McCall, PhD: Yes I would keep it in from the perspective of having people trust their practice of Boldness to discover they don't fall apart when they tell the truth out loud to another person. Whatever they were anticipating to come back as a response or reaction doesn't happen either. The exercise is practiced in a controlled setting where a sense of safety has been established. The point is they get to confront several things. One is their own fear, which they are already making up. And, they get to listen to what the other person has to say. Generally speaking these exercises have been fun. People enjoy them and, yes, I would keep it.

Tuck: I am reminded when I think about this exercise of another workshop I attended where we did something similar. As we were going around the circle, people were able to give feedback on their experience of me. It was fascinating for me to listen and receive what they were saying. For the first time, I was aware of myself listening, receiving and then choosing what I wanted to receive as true for me versus the projection of the other person onto me. Also I was aware that I was not getting triggered by what others were saying.

One woman shared with me that she found me to be extremely selfish. The other feedback was that I use humor to cover up certain aspects of myself. What I watched over the next 6 to 8 months was that the woman who said I was selfish left her husband behind in New York and followed our facilitator to another country. What it felt like was that she was focusing in on an aspect of my behavior that she wanted to express but was judging that behavior in herself.

Carol McCall, PhD: Whatever it was that she projected onto you was already in her. In her case, that would be selfishness, whatever the reason.

Tuck: It was fascinating to watch my response to hearing someone be very bold in how they experienced me.

Carol McCall, PhD: One of the things, one of the many things, I admire about you is that you're willing to put yourself in environments where people are not as conscious as you are.

Tuck: Maybe that's abusive. Am I abusing myself? (Laughing) I'm kidding.

Carol McCall, PhD: I think it is a legitimate question. Sometimes people will put themselves in a position in order to validate something. At one point in my life I went to workshops to validate that everyone else was not in the same "place" that I was.

When I went to a workshop with Eckhart Tolle, I went to be with him. I didn't go to be with the people in the workshop. The people in the workshop were just gushing over him. They thought that because I was there, that I was in the same place they were, in reference to how I felt about him. That wasn't it at all. Many people come to workshops to be with other people. I didn't come to be with other people. I came to be with him. That was bold.

One person asked me, "So what do you do?" I responded that I do workshops. Their response was, "Oh." I'm unwilling to put myself in a place where people are not really awake. If you're really awake, I'd spend time with you. And, you are welcome to give me all the feedback that you want.

Tuck: That's good Dr. C. So I wonder why Tuckie goes to workshops.

Carol McCall, PhD: Well, find out. What is your purpose? You have such a wealth of information. What's your purpose for being at the workshop? Are you still doing your research and gaining information? That's valid. If you are there for the workshop itself and you are learning something such as the structure and how it is being put together, that's valid. If you are learning ways to time certain things or how this information is going to be useful in terms of the work that you do, again, all of that is valid.

When participating in the exercise of people giving you feedback about you, it's important to know your purpose. You went through the exercise to get feedback. However to be curious about people's feedback when you are conscious, and you are clear that they are not conscious or you are clear on the level of their consciousness, take their feedback as part of the process of the exercise.

I regularly get feedback that I am arrogant. I get called arrogant because I choose to use the tool of being bold in my communication.

Tuck: I was at a workshop this weekend. I wanted to attend because I am thinking about partnering with one of the facilitators. I wanted to see how she works and facilitates her workshop. She happened to be co-leading with another woman. During the workshop the other woman took on the task of coaching me. I said to my friend after the workshop, "To attend workshops facilitated by you, Dr. C, Christian Pankhurst and Shavasti, the level of the work you all present is profoundly masterful."

I didn't feel safe in this workshop. I did not want this woman coaching me. I stood in complete silence for a while. I avoided her questions as long as I could, but she was insistent. I let her do what she wanted to do.

Carol McCall, PhD: Did you have an agreement to let her coach you?

Tuck: No

Carol McCall, PhD: Then you weren't bold. What was there for you to say that you didn't say? What was the truth?

Tuck: The truth was that I was very uncomfortable.

Carol McCall, PhD: The truth is you didn't feel safe, and you didn't tell her that. "I don't feel safe enough with you to let you coach me."

Tuck: It's okay to say that in front of the whole room?

Carol McCall, PhD: Absolutely it is. You could teach her something. She didn't ask permission to coach you did she?

Tuck: No she did not.

Carol McCall, PhD: Okay, then she opened herself up to that.

Tuck: That's really good.

Carol McCall, PhD: Unless she asked, she opened herself up to that. Unless she asked, "Do I have permission to coach you?" she didn't have your permission. She gets what she gets. How dare she assume she can coach you without asking your permission?

Unless there is an agreement in the workshop in writing that you agree to be coached, coaching is not appropriate.

You don't know me and I don't have that level of trust with you. Any coach who has been trained knows this. You have to ask permission. If you, as the participant, don't agree to it, now is the time to speak up. Otherwise you are agreeing to be coached.

Tuck: I've experienced you asking that very thing in your courses. You always ask, "Do I have permission to go there with you?"

Carol McCall, PhD: You don't do that to people without asking their permission.

Tuck: That's so good Dr. C. It seems so simple. Am I that unconscious? Am I that much in fear? See, I go to the Not Good Enough.

Carol McCall, PhD: You go to the fear of a reaction versus staying with the reality of what is happening.

Tuck: I was clear energetically what I was feeling. That was never the issue. I didn't go to the place of making myself wrong for what I was feeling. Where I went in my thinking was, "How dare I embarrass her in front of people?" I was stuttering. I couldn't respond. I know I stood there for a minute before I even said anything. She was trying to get me to talk about someone that I was uncomfortable talking about. I wasn't about to say anything about it in the workshop and she kept trying to get me to say it. I finally fabricated someone to get through the interaction.

Carol McCall, PhD: You began taking care of someone who had already violated your space. That's what you do Tuck. You take care of people who violate your space.

Tuck: I'm going to write that down.

Carol McCall, PhD: So wait a minute. They violated your space and you are taking care of them?

Tuck: That was the 3rd time she had done it. The first time she said out loud in the class, "Well Tuck it looks like you have something to say." The 3rd time she said that to me I asked if I had that written on my face because I clearly had nothing to say. I was sitting there listening. I'll talk when I am ready.

Ok, so I take care of people who violate my space.

Carol McCall, PhD: Now here is another level of subtlety going back to the Life Decision. In The Life Decision Not Good Enough/Better Than, you are Better Than showing her how really wrong she is. You are Better Than embarrassing her. (Laughing) You wouldn't stoop that low. You are Better Than that.

Tuck: Yes, there was a Better Than arrogant piece. In my mind I was thinking, how dare you, I have worked with Dr. Carol McCall, and I know what it feels like to be heard. That was the arrogant place I went to. And, it is true, Dr. C. (Laughing)

Carol McCall, PhD: The thing is that you were not bold in that moment, and we are talking about being bold. It was also useful for you to say to her, I have 3 coaches. They are so and so and so, and I don't allow other people to coach me. That would also have been a teaching moment for her.

Tuck: Yes, you know what happens to me? This is a great place for me to practice Boldness. When I get into those situations sometimes my mind goes blank. I'm uncomfortable. I don't want to make a scene. I can't figure out what to say. So out of fear of saying the wrong thing, that's when I start taking care of the other person.

You are really clear. I was not that clear. I am not that clear. How do I practice? Is there something I can say while I am composing myself? Or, do I say I am very uncomfortable

Carol McCall, PhD: Yes, I am very uncomfortable. I'm very uncomfortable with this interaction.

Tuck: That I can say. That will be bold.

Carol McCall, PhD: You can also say, "I am very unsafe in this interaction." That's really the truth.

Tuck: How interesting. There I was in an intuition class. This individual was teaching people to go within and trust their feelings. I felt uncomfortable in her coaching me and yet I said nothing. Boldness. What a subtle tool. It can sneak right by us. There is power in Boldness. It's interesting. That's what this Rebel Belle teaches. Boldness.

Carol McCall, PhD: We do teach that which we most need to learn. Thank you for this conversation today.

#6

INTUITION

A "LISTENING STYLE" THAT IS ALWAYS RIGHT.

Carol McCall, PhD: Our next tool of is Intuition, which is absolutely my favorite.

Tuck: Well that would make so much sense to Tuckie because in your Hologenetic Profile* (see Glossary) in the position of your Life's Work, you have the 57th Gene Key. The Gene Key of your Life's Work expresses the Gift of Intuition and your Highest Expression is Clarity.

Carol McCall, PhD: Wow. Well, I love being congruent.

When you reminded me the call was at 8 this morning, I set my alarm to be sure to wake up and make the call. If I was going to fall asleep, I was going to fall asleep on the phone here waiting for you. I was not going to miss this call. I wasn't sure if it was 8 your time or mine? I got on at 7 and you weren't there so I went shopping. I went shopping for shoes. I kept checking back every 15 or 20 minutes before realizing we were to meet at 8 my time, 9 your time.

What has this got to do with Intuition? Intuitively I have been paying attention to the results of the products I am now on for my thyroid. I'm keeping a record of what I'm taking. My thyroid is working differently now and I am shifting how I proceed through the day, especially in terms of my hunger. I have been able to complete some old patterns around food from way back when I was a little person.

I recall sitting at the dinner table and my grandmother Lucy Johnson saying to me, "Eat everything on your plate Carol Ann for the starving children in China." I'm clear that my weight has everything to do with all of the children that I ate for. So I ate for a lot of children so that they could remain thin. I remember at the table my little hunger mechanism would say "I'm full." I would say, "I'm full," to my grandmother and she would say, "eat everything on your plate," even beyond the time that I was full. I remember learning how to shut down and ignore the "full" signal.

Recently I was out to lunch and that signal came up that said, "I'm full." And the memory of what my grandmother taught me came back to me of learning how to shut down and ignore the full signal and continue to eat.

By the way, have I shared with you that I've had gastric by-pass surgery and now I don't ignore the signal?

Tuck: Yes

Carol McCall, PhD: I lost a huge amount of weight, and gained the majority of that back. I have been very disappointed with myself for having done that. I have forgiven myself. About 2 weeks ago I was channel surfing. I ran across TLC, The Learning Channel. They have this program called *My 600 Pound Life*. I was stopped by it. They had 4 people who had weighed close to 600 pounds. One of them died and was unable to participate. The other 3 have now lost half of their weight. They were down to about 150 or 180. My whole point was how many times I have yo-yoed up and down because I have ignored my intuition. I've ignored that signal that sends a message to the brain that says, "I'm full."

For this period of my life, I know that I will get back to my normal weight. I've never known what my normal weight is. I've yo-yoed so often. Intuitively I do know what my normal weight is. I've not ever honored it. So speaking of intuition, I know what to do. Intuitively I know how my body operates. I was a dancer from the age of 8 to 38. I know what my body requires. I'm now being returned back intuitively to knowing the difference between being hungry, thirsty and tired. What I have done the majority of my life is, that when that sensation would come, I would feed it, versus having water or exercising.

My body requires that I am physically active. Now, on top of all of that, I've always had a thyroid condition. I've known this for a very long time. I've checked in with Family Practitioners and asked them to check my thyroid. It always came up low, and they always refused to give me the medication. I'm now on the medication and it's making an enormous difference. As a matter of fact it has shifted my sleeping pattern. It is normal again. I go to sleep at 10. I get back up around 2. I go back to sleep and get back up around 6 in the morning. For me, this is normal.

Prior to that I would go to sleep in the middle of the day and not know when I was going to wake up. I started taking the thyroid medication and my whole system rebooted and changed. It restructured itself. I now remember my system, intuitively. It is time for me to truly honor and be my fully aligned authentic healthy self, whatever weight that is. I'm pretty sure it is about 150. I need to be respectful of what certain weight numbers look like on me. For me, 150 looks normal. I will now honor my body. It's all intuition.

When I don't trust my Intuition I really do get into trouble. When I do trust it I am fine. I have the thought I'm right. **And being right by trusting my intuition is one of the greatest epiphanies of my life. I feel so exhilarated. I'm happy, joyous. I hum.** All systems are aligned and on go. I'm on track and on purpose. Okay, then I ask myself, "How come you don't live there? How come you don't always trust your intuition all the time?" The answer is because I don't.

However, I live from my intuition, much more than I did when I was younger. I didn't live from my intuition in my 20's as much as I could have. I was right 100% of the time when I followed my intuition.

Now you've asked me how long I'm going to be in Chicago. I responded that I'll be here until May. That's intuitively what I got. I'm seeing San Diego. I've never lived there. I've visited there. I have an affinity for it. I'm seeing myself there, and I know that when I begin to see myself somewhere that's where I am to be. It's been wonderful to see myself there.

Intuition is 100% accurate all the time. There is no question that intuition works. It always works. **It doesn't work when I become analytical about Intuition. That's actually an oxymoron.** How can you be analytical about Intuition? **Logic and Intuition do not go together. That's the oxymoron.**

My favorite hero around that is Albert Einstein. He developed the Theory of Relativity intuitively. Of course, he had to go back and prove it for the left brained individuals who had no idea how to trust their Intuition. He had to prove the theory for the scientific community. He did.

Did you know that he flunked kindergarten? I love that. He was one of those children that couldn't deal with "the crap." I get it!

I trust my Intuition in terms of my move to San Diego, and in terms of my health. It isn't about weight anymore. It's about my health.

It isn't about my health so that something else will happen. There is no "so that". It's about my health. It's not that I'll lose weight "so that" I'll attract men, "so that" I look consistent with my brand, "so that" I'm credible, "so that" I can look like I'm from a certain class. This time it is to be healthy. I want to be healthy "so that", and this is the only "so that", I can live to be 101.

Tuck: Where does the 101 come from? Did you intuitively pick that?

Carol McCall, PhD: For many years it was 125, but now I don't want to live that long. With all the technology that exists, I trust that I can. But, I don't want to live until I'm 125.

Tuck: Talk to me about the statement "Intuition coupled with content allows for effectiveness and excellence in a timely manner." What does that mean as you have written it?

Carol McCall, PhD: Got it. When you intuit something, it's already right, whatever you are intuiting. Go back it up with information and content. When you act on it, it is efficient and effective. Intuitively you got the hit. Then you go and get the information to back it up. Then you act on it. It is a 100% go. It's going with the flow in a timely manner. That's how Albert Einstein did it. I love him. I'm going to have a picture of him in my office when I get to San Diego.

Tuck: I'm assuming we all come in with our Intuition fully aligned and intact. However, our Intuition is conditioned out of us at a very early age. How do we know when we are being intuitive?

Carol McCall, PhD: When you are being intuitive you are "in being". That's the only place Intuition lives, in being. Being IS Intuition. It doesn't have Intuition. It is Intuition. Once you access being, you don't have to DO anything to get somewhere. You ARE that state of being.

Tuck: Would you like to announce that to the world? Should we let the world in on our little secret? (Laughing)

Carol McCall, PhD: Once you access being, you are literally complete. You don't have to do anything. If you do anything, you are going to announce it to the world, like Eckhart Tolle did. He is 100% being. He is humor. He is nature. He is listening. He is all those things. When he answers questions, he answers from being information, not from having information. He is speaking it from being, not from something he learned. Being knows. It **is** Intuition.

You don't ever hear him say, "According to Dr. so and so, or on page 111, volume 4 paragraph 3." He never does that. He simply answers the question in an authentic, present way.

When we are listening, we are practicing mindful listening. Mindful listening is redundant, however. Right now when you are listening you are mindful, you are present in the moment. It means you are here. **When you are not here, you are hearing.**

People can quote verbatim word for word exactly what you say, but were they listening. Did they get the message on the mental, emotional, physical and spiritual level all at the same moment, one gestalt? Did they get that?

That's Empowered Mindful Listening™. When they hear me, did they get all 4 quadrants? Did they get it?

Generally speaking most people stay with their intellect and their feelings.

Tuck: I get the intellect. Talk to me about feelings. How does that get in the way?

Carol McCall, PhD: Their feelings are either I like it or I don't like it. Those are their feelings. They receive the information through their intellect. Then they sift it through the filter of their feelings. They either like it or they don't. It's a sensation they feel about it. It's their feelings. I agree with you or I don't agree with you. It impacts their feelings.

However, they don't bother to go to the spirituality of it. They don't bother dealing with the physicality of it. They don't deal with the nuances or the vibration. How did the vibration hit you? How did the words impact you? They don't go there. They know that it happened. However, they don't really take in that

moment in time. I heard the message. The words you used to deliver it didn't work. It created other sensations in my body. Intuitively what did you get? Frequently most people can answer that intuitively what they got is that you are scared.

Fear is a condition. When babies are born under glaring lights being smacked by the doctor to get their first breath they learn fear. Fear is conditioned.

Since we are part of the animal kingdom, we instinctively recognize danger. When we do, we take appropriate action. We either fight or flight. Instinctively we get that it's about survival. All species have the survival instinct.

However, we are conditioned to be afraid of things we don't need to be afraid of. For instance, I'm conditioned to be afraid of someone's opinion. Are you kidding? I'm conditioned to be afraid of thinking a certain way or of saying certain things. I'm conditioned to be afraid of certain people's looks. That's conditioned. Prior to that, as a child, all I am is curious. I'm a sponge learning all kinds of things. I get things intuitively.

I feel much safer with babies and children than I do with anyone past the age of 13. Past this age they have been conditioned and are busy putting up their barriers, defense mechanisms and façades. They are busy building their personalities. It's a tough row to hoe being an adolescent. These years are learning by trial and error. Adolescents are the harshest critics of themselves and each other. How come people go back to their high school reunions is still a mystery to me.

Tuck: I so agree with you.

Carol McCall, PhD: You are going back to your 10th or 20th reunion, for what?

Tuck: To see if I can handle it? (Laughing)

When we are in being we are essence. We are aligned and connected. I'm curious, when I read you the words, Clarity, Intuition, Awakening, Expansion, Superabundance, and Ascension do they sound like the essence of your being to you. These are your essence words in Human Design. They represent the quality of your consciousness. When I say those words to you do they sound like *the being* of who you are?

Carol McCall, PhD: Yes.

Tuck: Clarity, Intuition, Expansion, and Superabundance. Being feels so good. Any outflow of those essence words through you, can't help but be filled with love, bounteousness and lack of judgment. What is there to judge?

Carol McCall, PhD: The word Superabundance is interesting to me. I have been in an investigative mode with myself about how come I don't get something. What it is that I don't get is this. I've been getting feedback recently with individuals asking, "How can you live in an Executive Apartment fully furnished?" That makes you homeless. I don't get it. I don't get that I'm homeless. I've heard the comment a couple of times particularly from my family members. They'll share, "Carol you've been homeless for quite a while." I've never been homeless. My daughter tells me she never wants to be homeless. I tell her she won't be. She is not.

Whatever homeless is, it's just not a possibility for me.

Tuck: I've had the privilege of traveling around the country in an RV and staying in RV parks. Some might refer to the RV lifestyle as homeless. As a person from South Carolina, the mobile home capital of the world, I had in my mind that an RV park was like a trailer park. My opportunity to experience this lifestyle

changed my perspective forever. People living this lifestyle are filled with a sense of freedom and peace and they are in being because they are not strapped with a home.

As you know, I've sold my house. I don't own a home right now. We are living temporarily with my son. When people tell me I, too, am homeless, I say, "Oh no, I am home free. I am not homeless. I don't know that I want to own a home."

Carol McCall, PhD: Exactly. That's why I'd like to own an apartment building. I don't want to own a home. I want to own an apartment building so the management can take care of it. (Laughing) I'm willing to assume that responsibility of owning the building. For me this is being home free.

Tuck: There is nothing in your chart that says you should ever do anything that looks like conformity. (Laughing) You do it with your own exquisite style. Isn't that using your Intuition and allowing yourself to create it as you go?

McCall: Yes. It's playing a bigger game. Your brother made a comment to me the other day about being bored and not playing a bigger game. That's really not the thing to say to me. Anyone who is bored is not playing a big enough game. They are operating under the thought-form of "who am I to give my gifts to the world?" How dare you not? You signed up to. It is arrogant not to. That's not keeping your word. Get up off of your butt and go deliver it.

Tuck: Interesting. I have a friend who is always telling me she is bored. Not too long ago she was also sharing how she was not speaking up in a group call the way she wanted to. She actually said, "Who am I to?" So, when she shared she was bored with her life, I responded to her that was borderline arrogant.

Carol McCall, PhD: It is arrogant. She agreed to come here for a reason. Now she has reneged. How does she feel about people who don't keep their promises?

Tuck: She says she is even bored with her friends.

Carol McCall, PhD: She is bored with her friends because she projects onto them what she is not doing. If you are hanging out with people and you are bored, these are people keeping you in your boredom. She has picked her environment very carefully to keep her bored, to keep her limited and arrogant.

Tuck: What about me? I'm one of her friends. Do I keep her bored?

Carol McCall, PhD: No! You are not in her face all of the time about her delivering her gift.

Tuck: Interesting. So how come she is in seclusion?

Carol McCall, PhD: She is in hiding. She is scared to deliver her gift. Somewhere she has sold out. Going back to the question for her, how does she feel about people who do not keep their word?

Tuck: It pisses her off.

Carol McCall, PhD: That's because that is what she does. She pisses off a lot of people around her. To be locked up into that thought form of "who am I to" is huge. You are the person who signed on to come here to deliver your gift. That's who you are.

Tuck: Again, interesting, because when this woman is aligned with her being, she is love, acceptance, heart, devotion. When she is not holding back I feel her full presence, her life force.

Carol McCall, PhD: When you are being intuitive you are "in being". That's the only place Intuition lives, in being. Being IS Intuition. It doesn't have Intuition. It is Intuition. Once you access being, you don't have to DO anything to get somewhere. You ARE that state of being.

#7

99:1/MSU

A LISTENING AND SPEAKING STYLE THAT IS ALWAYS SOMETHING "MADE UP" ABOUT THE PAST OR FUTURE.

Carol McCall, PhD: 99:1/MSU is one of my favorite most often referred to tools in Empowered Mindful Listening™. Especially now that I'm really emphasizing Empowered Mindful Listening™, it requires that I be absolutely mindful in terms of when I'm making stuff up. When I have the thought of someone and a feeling comes with that thought, it's important to become even more present to 99:1/MSU. Simply the thought of something can trigger me. I'm now in the past or the future. All that happened was to have a thought about it and a feeling comes with it. The concept of a thought followed by a feeling is valid.

What I'm excited about is that now I'm engaged in the brain wave research project. This research provides the opportunity to actually see on a graph each and every thought that I have. That demonstrates their validity.

For example, I'm having a thought about my Aunt right now. The very fact that I thought of her was immediately followed by a feeling.

Tuck: That's funny. I could feel the shift in the vibration immediately.

And, there is no "of course" when you're Making Stuff Up since MSU appears to be real. Unless there really is information and action that demonstrates a reality about whatever the thought is that you had or have about the person, place or thing, and you check it out, you cannot be present to what is so. (INDENT)

Carol McCall, PhD: All I have to say is Aunt. I don't even have to say her name anymore. I have a lot made up about her. Some of it isn't made up. I've been here for a year in the area where she lives. So, now I have information. I have facts.

However, all I have to do is bring up the words, "my Aunt", and there it is. My whole energy shifts. What is it that I've made up? 99:1 is about what I've made up. What I've made up about her is that I'm not safe with her. I become angry. My anger has to do with the fact that for many years I idolized her. She was like my big sister. I looked up to her. I wanted to be like her. She was popular. She ran in this exclusive group of women. I wanted to be like her for years.

My experience with my Aunt has now shifted. It shifted when my mother went into retirement. My Aunt owned her apartment building, which we thought was great. It was a guaranteed shelter for family members. If we didn't have our own home we could always go live with my Aunt. My mother was the first person to whom she said no. She told her she had to go live elsewhere.

What I had made up about my Aunt became distorted. I was shattered. She wasn't the person that I had made her up to be.

What is so in this particular moment is, "Do I feel safe with my Aunt?" In this particular moment the answer is no. The minute I say her name I leave. I go to the past. I go to when she turned down my mother's request to live with her when she retired. I don't even stay present.

How come I don't stay present? It's a result of the fantasy I had built up around my Aunt. Now as I stay present with you, I am in touch with my sadness. I'm sad about it. It's almost to the point where I am ready to cry. It is a loss. What is the loss? The loss is of the fantasy that I made up about my Aunt. I made up a fantasy about my Aunt. Then I made up that I wanted to be like this fantasy.

Tuck: This might be a lofty way of looking at this. Unless I am truly present, willing to allow and accept the experience in the moment and perhaps express from that experience, everything is made up. When I read about the New Human, I move into the space of self-reflected awareness, where I am aware that I am experience experiencing itself, otherwise EVERYTHING is made up. Mindfulness is huge. I suppose we have to ask ourselves in each moment, am I present?

Carol McCall, PhD: I'm smiling because here's another piece. If we have to ask, "Am I present?" then we are not present. (Laughing) In the present moment we don't have to ask, "Am I present?"

Tuck: I know, and 99:1, that is a huge percentage of Made Up Stuff to real stuff.

Carol McCall, PhD: Recently I was in a store and there was this adorable little baby lying in this basket. It was looking right at me. I said to the baby, "Welcome." This baby was present, like, "Hello." I said, "Welcome." The baby was here in this moment. It was awesome to see that level of presence.

Very often this is so when I look at children particularly up to the age of 3. At 4 or 5 they begin to develop the rudiments of the personality they are going to live from, that thought they make up about themselves. The Life Decision is pretty much ingrained by the time we are 5. As a 3 year old it is still up for grabs. It's not solidified yet. At 3 there is still presence. They are still inquisitive working to figure it all out. It is delightful to be in the presence of presence. We lose it for a substantial part of time in our life.

It is what you said, 99:1. 99% of the time we are Making Stuff Up. That 1% where we are not, that's reality. My thought is to have us reverse this, for 99% of the time to have us be present and 1% of the time Making Stuff Up. Wouldn't that be great? When we are listening, mindfully listening, we are present. We are in the present moment. In the present moment there is nothing there except the experience of being.

Then of course the human ego comes in and accuses us of being self-absorbed. In the present moment what else is there?

Tuck: That's a great question, "What else is there?"

Carol McCall, PhD: It's certainly not the ego.

Tuck: It's a whole new experience for most of us isn't it? I had an experience this weekend around purchasing a new home. I asked myself, "Am I attached to getting this particular house?" In this moment I'm feeling joy, passion and excitement. I'm feeling aligned with the essence of this home. If we get it, fabulous! If not, I trust something else that is good will come to us. I'm in the place of being present. I'm trusting that in staying present we will get what we need versus going into the fears about our survival. Still, at times there is a part of me that wants to throw a temper-tantrum if I don't get what I want. So this weekend, I sat on the front porch of the condo taking in the view of the ocean, alone in silence, attempting to still myself and be mindful, or not. Sometimes I wonder if the reason my body feels so tired is because I can't shut off my thinking. My mind works so hard to solve the problems of my life.

Carol McCall, PhD: In the present moment you don't have any problems.

Tuck: It sounds so simple. How do we live in our world if everyone is a walking 99%? How are we communicating?

Carol McCall, PhD: We are not. We are talking. We are hearing and, for the most part, we are not communicating. We are not speaking and listening. By listening I mean choosing each word that comes out of our mouths. We are not listening as in listening to all four quadrants: mental, physical, emotional and spiritual. We are not listening to ourselves. We are not listening to the other. We are not listening. We are not mindful of the full gestalt of the message we are receiving and what we are doing with it.

Am I feeling cold? Am I processing it? Am I putting weight on each word that person says to me? What does that word mean to that person? How am I listening to the speaker?

Two things come up for me. One is the word compassion. The other is the word "weighting". What I mean by "weighting" is putting a certain intensity/emphasis to that word. You were speaking a minute ago about waiting, as in giving space to things between us. Maybe the word "weighting" is to be translated into the words Empowered Mindful Listening™, which means listening in all 4 quadrants, physical, mental, emotional, spiritual. In my own experience in listening to others, we are so ready to get on with the conversation. Wouldn't it serve to stop, slow down, and really be clear that what I'm hearing you say is what you're intending to say to me? You might even care enough to ask me how I'm receiving your words.

Tuck: That takes time.

Carol McCall, PhD: It takes practice. It's not so much time as it is practice. I have the thought that when people say it takes time that they mean it takes time to practice. My daughter and I always check in with one another by asking, "How did you hear what I just said?"

It doesn't take time to ask the question. However, I'm checking to be sure that the way I'm delivering this message is really getting through to her as the listener. "How are you hearing what I just said?" Or, I will ask, "What are you doing with what I just said?"

I particularly do this as her mother. One of the filters she processes me through is called Mom. I don't always want her to hear me as Mom. Sometimes I want her to listen to me as another woman talking to her. I respect her. Frequently she becomes my baby. I'm not talking to her as my baby, but as another woman. I make sure I choose the words that regularly bring with it the energy of talking to an adult. I am being responsible for the words I choose when I speak with her.

I recently noticed how I have been speaking to my son as if he were a little boy when I say, "Hi Raleigh." I stopped doing this. He is not a boy. He is a grown man. In my heart he is still my little boy, so this, "Hi Raleigh" tone, while I mean it lovingly, doesn't come across lovingly.

I checked myself for the truth. I got my salutation was for the little boy. So now it's, "Hi Raleigh – Hello." My voice is full. I am greeting a full grown adult. It has everything to do with not making anything up about him. I'm greeting him. We are face-to-face and adult-to-adult. I got my job done. I'm very proud of him as a man. So I greet him as an adult, a grown man, and in my heart I am talking to my little boy.

He will always be my little boy in my heart. I simply don't need to interact with him that way, period.

I had a past life regression reading years ago. I loved it. There was a time when I was doing regression sessions. It was in California. I would go to these workshops of past life regressions. They were absolutely fascinating. In one of the sessions my son had also been my husband, my father, my brother and my boss. Now in this life, in terms of an energetic connection, he is my son. I may choose to come back or not. If I do, I wonder what he will be the next time. My daughter has also been my mother, my sister, my aunt and my best friend. Those were the life regressions I had the opportunity to experience.

Going back to Making Stuff Up, 99:1/MSU, does that impact how I interact with each of them now? Really, what difference does it make, as long as I'm interacting authentically with them in each present moment?

What are we making up when we are listening? A lot gets made up while we're listening, according to researchers. Let's make sure we do our part to practice having people be 99% present and only 1% distracted. Can you imagine what a world that would be?

I have the thought that we may eventually evolve into that.

I notice my granddaughter's presence. She is 21 and very present. When she looks at me she is here. It is a surprise because I don't experience people that often being as present as she is. Now I've come to expect her to be present. There is no falseness between us. She requires my presence and I give it. She and my daughter are like two little glue pads they are so present to each other. I have to work to interrupt them because they are that present to one another.

That's what I would anticipate, that we would all be so connected and close to each other, that this would be a world of inclusion rather than exclusion. We would be interdependent. It would be a natural thing for us to help anyone who required assistance and support. If you saw someone fall down of course you would go and help them to get up. If you saw someone coming through the door, of course you would open the door. It becomes an "of course". If you see someone, of course you would say hello. Whether you know them or not you would say hello because you do know them.

It would be a shift in our paradigm about being, and being with people. It's welcoming another human being. It would be that 99% of the people are present. Then there would be 1% who are distracted. These people would be in a sanatorium. They would be insane because they are not here. Anyone who is sane is present. People who are not present are considered insane. What a switch. Sanity is being sane. Sanity is being present. Insanity is being distracted, disoriented and not here. Based on this thought we live in an insane world. Well, yeah we do. That brings me full circle back to my aunt. No wonder I don't feel safe with her, she is "insane".

Tuck: There was a point there as you were talking where I felt deep emotion. You and I have spoken before of that place of emotion. It's that place where we can feel God. Imagine living from a place that feels that full. I think you said lovingly and humorously last week, this listening and allowing of the life force energy is too much for this little human vessel to hold. Imagine having it flipped so that we are coursing 99% of life force energy, listening energy, through this tiny little vessel. I might explode. (Laughing)

Carol McCall, PhD: I have the thought that our vessel would expand to hold it. The thought that I had was that our bodies are already holding it and we're waiting for the opportunity to expand into our fullness and this is the appropriate body for it. We come in different shapes, forms and sizes. As I look at Hollywood, we have these huge energies in these little tiny bodies and in these big, tall bodies. It's all big energy.

Tuck: Do you get that about your book, this little tiny book that people will be holding in their hands? Imagine what it is holding, the energy and the spirit it's holding. Very exciting!

Carol McCall, PhD: Speaking of this book I was Amazon shopping the other day. I was looking at their services. We could sell it on Amazon. Have you thought about where we could sell it?

Tuck: I would have to go back to my notes in conversation with Philippe. He gave me a couple of different possibilities depending on how we wrote the book; on demand or digital download. I assume we could do both.

Carol McCall, PhD: We can self publish through Amazon. They take a percentage. I want the book out there. What am I willing to give up for that, as long as it is our book? That's not the only place we can sell it. In terms of exploring, this is good, as long as I am not limited to selling it there. They say, "Come be in business with us." It's great!

As we were in conversation, I didn't Make Up anything about Amazon. I did have the thought about ownership. I had the thought about distribution; however, I didn't make up anything about it. That was freeing as a possibility of one avenue in terms of getting the book out. It was all in the space of what is possible. I have the thought now, living 100% in the present moment, that there was a lot of space around it. That was very freeing. Even with Philippe, he was information. There was nothing rigid.

When we live without making anything up (99:1/MSU) people can live as resources. They are valuable. They can contribute.

What's important is Empowered Mindful Listening™ and making sure that my environment is calm and high vibrating so that I stay present and there is no MSU.

#8

COMPLETION

A LISTENING AND SPEAKING STYLE THAT ALLOWS THE LISTENER AND SPEAKER TO MOVE TO THE NEXT EVENT WITH A FULL FOCUS/ PRESENCE.

Carol McCall, PhD: So here we are at the tool of Completion, which is "satisfaction in the present moment." Practicing the tool of Completion is something I have truly been engaged in for the experience of bringing myself to satisfaction in the present moment. Also, recognizing that when I am dissatisfied in the moment I am not complete and I am not in that present moment.

I was watching one of my TV shows which I will often do, allowing myself to go mindless and be entertained and get caught up in the drama of the show. Watching TV is also a way I continue to enjoy studying human behavior. Writers are absolutely brilliant with their dialog and conversations. I pay close attention to the current conversation and language being used for people to connect. When I discover and am brought present to, "I am not satisfied right now," it's from the perspective that I'm not even in the present moment right now. If I were in the present moment right now I would be in the dynamic and the energy that the TV dialog has designed for me.

One of my favorite shows to watch is the talent show *The Voice*. I intuitively know who is going to be picked. When I find myself dissatisfied it's when I get that I'm attached to a particular person rather than being present to whatever is happening on the show. I become attached. The minute I become attached, I am no longer present. I am dissatisfied, so I'm not complete.

What I'm clear about now is how attachment is a major source of my stress and incompletion and lack of satisfaction. Attachment definitely takes me out of the moment. In the present moment there is nothing for me to be attached to.

Tuck: It's interesting. When I hear the word Completion, what comes to mind is the word "finished". You talk about your attachment creating an incompletion. This is interesting. When people tell me they are bored, I interpret that as an incompletion from the perspective that their boredom is their excuse to quit and give up on something before it's complete. They are tired of not reaching their intended outcome in their timing so they give up. They say they are bored. They don't finish or complete what they began.

Carol McCall, PhD: That's beautiful. When people tell me they are bored my first response is that they don't have enough to do in their life. They are not playing a big enough game if they are bored. They aren't even present to life when they are bored.

Tuck: Map this on. When we are bored we are incomplete. We are not playing a big enough game. I'm looking at your description of the tool of Completion here, and it reads: "Completion allows us to move on to the next event with full focus on the next event." In being incomplete and bored something must be going on in that present moment where we are either regretting our past or worrying about our future.

Carol McCall, PhD: All of the above. The key is they are not in the present moment. People who are in the present moment are not bored.

Tuck: There is a lot of vitality in your statement.

Carol McCall, PhD: It takes stamina to stay present since the human ego moves so quickly. There is an imitation of "being present", and that is doing this and doing that and doing something else. That is an imitation of being present. That's the ego's imitation of being present. That's not being present; as a result, there is no fulfillment.

Tuck: The ego's imitation of being present, which cannot be satisfaction in the present moment, is because they are seeking something.

Carol McCall, PhD: Exactly. They are not fulfilled. They are not mindful. Empowered Mindful Listening™ means one is present, here, focused.

Tuck: Completion means one has gone as far as one can, given the situation for now. I'm thinking about this for two reasons. You taught my daughter that in the heat of the moment when we are not listening to one another any longer, we are caught up in the drama. What would work is for one of us to ask for a break or a pause. We are complete for that moment. We can revisit it later, and we are complete in that moment. That's clear communication.

The second situation is this. When I was a participant in "The Rebel Road" tour with Simran, what I heard her say was this: "I have gone as far as I can go being who I am. Yes, I have been the publisher and editor of a magazine. I have hosted my own radio show. I've experienced myself in fulfillment of these things. I am complete. Now, what I'd like to do is step off into the abyss. I want to step forward onto a blank canvas. I want to experience myself as something I've never experienced before."

When I shared, earlier in our conversation, that there is a lot of vitality in this tool, this is what I was referring to. Completion is being in the present moment and letting everything be.

Carol McCall, PhD: There is a quote that I love. I'll see if I'm able to remember it correctly. I'll make every effort not to cry. **"To be willing to give up at any moment what I have become in order to be what's possible."** (Author unknown).

Tuck: I'm writing this down. I'm getting chills.

Carol McCall, PhD: I'm not recalling the author. I do know I heard it from Werner. It wasn't his and I heard him say it. It is still with me. Every time I recall it, it brings me to tears. I was in tears when I heard it from him. It moves me to my core.

Completion really moves you to give up, to let go of, what you have become, in order to be what's possible. Now, this is in every moment. This is as far as you can go. Mapping this on to Simran saying, "I want to step into the abyss", this is letting go of what she has become, as far as she can go now, in order to be what's possible.

That is true transformation. People talk transformation. They do not walk transformation. Transformation means having no idea how we are going to turn out on the other side. We have no idea, no road map for it. We have no immediate or close role models for it. We can't say, "My mother is like that or my sister is like that," since there is no one out there in our personal relationship circle modeling transformational behavior. We become the canvas. We become the blueprint. It's within us. We simply have no idea since we have never seen it before. We've never seen anyone like us before. How come? Fact! There is no one like us. We are each unique. Our transformation is individually unique to each of us.

The only person I have seen actively reinvent herself is Madonna. This woman masterfully reinvents herself. She is complete with what was and moves to the "what's next." She is constantly evolving, working it and practicing it.

Completion is about going as far as you can for now in the situation. Let's consider people who are beginning their path of self-development. It is no longer a good idea to be who they are. This is a Completion and now they are embarking on Self-Development 101.

How does one explain Completion to someone in Self-Development 101? Give them the information, which

is that this is as far as you have the presence to go right now. Call for a break since this is as much of the conversation as they can handle right now. We'll get back to the conversation in two minutes, hours, days or years. Assist them to understand this is as far as they can go for now.

Tuck: How does the human condition allow Completion for now to happen? I am a processor. I love self-examination. What is the piece of information that would serve so that I don't spend all of my time processing so I can be complete for now and give my full focus somewhere else? Mind doesn't allow me to do that sometimes.

Carol McCall, PhD: Speaking of the human condition, the ego must hang on, which is living in the past. **The only ways the human ego can exist are in the past and/or play "what if" which is the future. It has no existence in the present moment.**

Tuck: I love the "what if."

Carol McCall, PhD: "What if" is the future. I don't live in the future with others when I'm coaching them, unless I say, "Okay let's play what if." What I'm really doing is having the person shift to possibility to get them dislodged from a rigid way of thinking. A lot of people don't like to play in possibility, so we play in "what if."

They will go there. They won't go to the possibility of other possibilities. I go as far as the human ego let's me go. It doesn't know what I'm doing. I know what I'm doing. I had a coaching session this morning where I asked, "What's the possibility?" The response was, "There is no possibility." I said again, "Anything is possible." Repeat after me, "Anything is possible." The client refused to repeat the statement saying it was not true that anything is possible. So then I went to "what if" to which the client responded, "Okay, yes, that's possible." That was how I had to play that to get the client dislodged from the rigidity of their thinking. The human ego of the client was holding onto the past.

Tuck: Now that would require presence to navigate this conversation, yes? (Laughing)

Carol McCall, PhD: After about 20 minutes I had gone as far as was possible in the present moment with that person and I said, "You know this is as far as we can go with this in the present moment, are you complete for now?" The client's response was, "Yes, I am and there is a lot of freedom right now."

Tuck: In some of the other tools we've talked about, specifically Empowered Mindful Listening™, when Empowered Mindful Listening™ is present in a conversation, I have the thought that there is a greater chance for Completion. When it is not present, there is no Empowered Mindful Listening™ and, therefore, no clear communication. I'm thinking specifically about myself when I go unconscious in my conversations. It's then that I exhibit the behavior of needing to be right, in the conversation. All the tools of Empowered Mindful Listening™ serve in bringing Completion to our conversations. I'm present. I'm not attached to being right. I'm listening mindfully.

Carol McCall, PhD: All of these tools are actually actions that strengthen our ability to be focused and present. That is exactly what these tools do. They strengthen our conversations and capacity to be present.

Tuck: That could be a tag line for your Nine Tools of Empowered Mindful Listening™, "How to Strengthen Your Ability To Be Present" or something like that. The words "present" and "being present" are big buzzwords these days. The Nine Tools of Empowered Mindful Listening™ provide a deeper definition for the word presence.

Carol McCall, PhD: Yes, each tool strengthens one's ability to be present. It's rich. Elizabeth Claire Prophet used to say, "Completion is the all-ness of God." To which I say, "Yay!" She said that at the end of many of her lectures.

Tuck: I might have to steal that from Elizabeth Claire Prophet. When I finish my calls I can say, "We are complete, and Completion is the all-ness of God."

Carol McCall, PhD: When I'm not sure where people are in their spirituality, I will say, "Completion is the all-ness of the Universe." People get it. Everyone can hear Universe. Even my wonderful client Hunt Self let's me say that.

Tuck: That makes Tuck laugh. It's so nice of him to allow you to say that. (Laughing)

Carol McCall, PhD: I love that man. He is wonderful. We have great coaching sessions.

Tuck: May I share what feels like a Completion for me with you? I was going through Facebook today looking at pictures. There was a beautiful picture of my brother at my Aunt's funeral, with my two sisters sitting on his lap. I looked at it, the first feeling and thought was, "That's really sweet, and he doesn't have to take care of me anymore." It was interesting. That feels like Completion. I don't need him to take care of me. I'm not his little sister anymore. The relationship is different.

Carol McCall, PhD: Even with your Completion, with his no longer taking care of you, it is now a different energy for you. He can continue taking care of you as his little sister. It will feel different to you.

Tuck: When he was here, he and Larry and I went to dinner. Then he, my son and I spent some time together. The energy was full, respectful. It was different and felt right.

Carol McCall, PhD: He is a real treasure. I feel privileged, blessed, and joyful that I get to coach him. It's a great experience to coach him.

Tuck: He does not trust people easily. That's a testament to your ability to create safe, psychic space for people, a safe haven for people to do their work.

Carol McCall, PhD: In terms of Completion did you have your Group call? You had asked me about that.

Tuck: I did.

Carol McCall, PhD: Are you complete?

Tuck: For now.

Carol McCall, PhD: Do you have satisfaction that the event took place, and you're satisfied in the moment?

Tuck: Yes.

Carol McCall, PhD: Good. You are complete.

I'd like to give us some homework. Our homework is to declare Completion. Now, I do practice Completion, and I commit to practice more. This morning I made dinner. I had all my food in the slow cooker. I have 3 different parts to my meal, and they are all slow cooking so that they will be ready by 5 o'clock this evening. I was complete once everything was put into the separate crockpots. I actually said, "I'm complete." I am satisfied. Dinner preparation is now out of the way. Now I'm ready for my calls. I can be completely present as a result of preparing dinner ahead of time.

Tuck: Practice makes permanent. Did someone say that one day? (Laughing)

Carol McCall, PhD: Yes. Author unknown. I've been using it ever since. Practice makes permanent.

Tuck: On another note, I just googled and found the quote you spoke about earlier. The Tao Te Ching reads, "When I let go of what I am, I become what I might be. When I let go of what I have, I receive what I need."

That's what I just found in my Google search.

Carol McCall, PhD: Perhaps that's where Werner found it. That would make sense. It's a beautiful passage to complete our tool of Completion.

#9

COACH ACTION- STOP THE DRAMA

A LISTENING AND SPEAKING STYLE THAT "STOPS-THE-DRAMA" IN AN INTERACTION.

Carol McCall, PhD: Here we are with our last tool for Empowered Mindful Listening™, Coach Action-Stop the Drama: What is an action I wouldn't normally take? When I ask people the question, "What is an action you wouldn't normally take?" they will usually say that they do not know. This is true for them. They don't know because they are usually so caught up in the drama that it doesn't occur to them that there is an action they would not normally take.

Since I have been doing this work for so long, I have a number of different actions that I take that I wouldn't normally take. I announce the drama. I escalate the drama. I stop, I catch it and I communicate out loud. These are all actions I wouldn't normally take (laughingly) since I am this trained, enlightened being, right?

What else would I not normally do? The answer varies. Recently as I have found myself headed in the direction of drama I've stopped and said, "No, I'm not doing that one." The most recent thing I've done in terms of Coach Action and stopping the drama is, I read one of my many quotes by Abraham about attraction and how having negative thoughts attracts negative experiences. This one was about money. I begrudge others who have money. The thoughts were, "How come they are making all that money. How come they are on the Internet with thousands of people?" Those very thoughts keep abundance away from me.

I've been checking that kind of comparison and thought process in terms of, well, if Steve Harrison or Deepak Chopra can do it, so can I. I've been stopping that question. By comparing, it keeps me locked into a limited way of thinking. This is an action I wouldn't normally take, to stop the comparisons and to get that by even making comparisons, that very thought process, keeps abundance away from me. It attracts negativity and limitation.

Whatever I can't be with, doesn't allow me to rid myself of it. It is an incompletion. "What I resist persists." I learned that from Werner. If I can't be with the success of Wayne Dyer, Deepak Chopra or Dr. Phil, or any of the other gurus, I'm keeping my own success away from me. So I can stop, stop the thought pattern. Now that's normally an action I would not take. That's what I have been doing recently. Stop the thoughts. Stop the drama. Those thoughts are nothing more than drama. I have enough coming at me. I don't need to create the drama. When I stand still, when I am present there is plenty of drama. Then I look at, what are the kinds of thoughts I'm having that would attract this kind of energy to come at me?

Werner would say, "How am I being that this is happening in my space?" Asking this question has always been a useful practice for me. This is about Coach Action-Stop the Drama: Taking an action I would not normally take.

While I see that people are a "drama waiting to happen," I am part of the people.

Tuck: So, you're practiced with this tool of Coach Action-Stop the Drama and therefore might catch yourself in drama before others do. When someone is in their drama around anything and, therefore, not present, how do they stop the drama if they don't know they are not present and in drama?

Carol McCall, PhD: I'll answer that by giving you a very short story. Throughout the month my body wants certain foods. Recently it has wanted three different kinds of foods: pizza, Pastrami Ruben Sandwiches and the third one is a burrito. I went to my favorite burrito restaurant, Chipotle, to order. As I was going through the line, the woman behind the counter was busy doing her service thing. "Would you like this, would you like this, would you like this?" I said to her, "Slow down." She was really in the drama of making sure she was getting everything just right. She looked at me and she let out a huge exhale. Then she said slowly, "Would you like some of this?" She literally slowed down.

Tuck: You just boldly said, "Slow down?"

Carol McCall, PhD: Yes, that's what I said, "Slow down." I wasn't going to buy into her drama. I wasn't going to be rushed or to speed up to her pace. Clearly she was in drama because she was "busy being busy" and making sure that she was efficient. From the perspective that I am sensitive to others' energy, I have no problem managing their energy around me. I don't buy into their energy. I will deliberately slow down around people like this, when they are in drama. This action I do a lot since most people today are busy being busy.

Fortunately, when they are my clients, I have permission to do that. When they are not my clients, I give myself permission to do it. It's about me making sure I don't buy into their stuff.

Tuck: What I was listening for was answered when you said something like, "I can't be with the piece around money with other people." I have that same kind of response around others' behavior and their lack of presence. That's the inquiry I have been on this morning. I've said to myself, "Okay, since this particular behavior is in my energy field, my state of mind is actually creating this external circumstance."

This week I had an experience on a call where I went into drama. The call topic was about presence and being present. My energy was rattled as one individual began talking about the drama in her life. She talked 100 miles an hour. She had a nervous giggle in her communication and kept repeating, "It's all good. It's all good."

I'm curious as to whether this was about drama within me and how I am to handle it within my listening. Or, is it more about being bold and handling something externally?

Carol McCall, PhD: Something similar happened to me at a restaurant. The person wasn't talking to me. They were talking a mile a minute and their leg was shaking as if they had palsy. I said to my daughter, "That woman's mind is racing a mile a minute. Just watching her is causing anxiety for me, so I'm no longer going to watch her. I am going to put my focus elsewhere. I am going to focus on what I came here to get. I am going to take a deep breath." That's what I did.

I don't buy that I always attract things. I do accept that in the environment things show up. How I respond to them has everything to do with my state of being. The whole world literally is anxious. This is not news. So I don't say, "How come I am attracting anxiousness?" I'm not attracting it. I am in a place where there is anxiety. If I don't like it I can always go somewhere else.

Tuck: So what I am discerning is that I go into drama about how I am affected by that anxiety. I'm looking to stop the drama about what my reaction is, as opposed to having a healthy response, meaning making or choosing a conscious response, which is what I am hearing that you do. You have a conscious healthy response to it. I apparently am still in the drama of being a victim of how the circumstance affects me. Does that make sense?

Carol McCall, PhD: Yes, I don't let someone else's energy affect me. For me, I compare it to body odor. If someone has body odor, I don't think I attract it. They have the body odor. What am I going to do about it? Well, I'm going to remove myself as quickly as possible.

Tuck: Okay, great guru of mine, can you support me here? When you are facilitating, say, your

"Possibility of Woman" (POW) * workshop, and there is a woman with body odor in the room, do you do anything? In this group I participate in, I am the facilitator.

You used to say that it takes a lot to hold the structure and the energy of a group, when people are learning to be present. No wonder I still feel as if I am getting hooked into the drama within myself.

Carol McCall, PhD: You are getting hooked with the fact that there is all this energy, and asking, "What do I do about it? I don't like it." Instead, observe and say, "Ah, there is all this energy. Let me hold the space." It has nothing to do with you. Simply hold the space.

Tuck: When you have permission to coach and give feedback, my experience of how you work and facilitate is *that* much more powerful since there's a willingness to listen and a possibility of action for the client.

Carol McCall, PhD: Even when I don't have permission to coach them, I will say, "Will you please slow down? I really want to hear what you have to say and right now I'm not able to hear all of what you are saying. Will you please slow down?" I don't have an issue with saying that. I put it on them. "I want to hear everything you have to say and right now I'm not able to follow you. Would you slow down?"

I'm telling them about what is so for me in the moment. "You are going awfully fast. I'm not able to stay with you. Would you slow down so that I can be with you? I really want to hear this." That's as much control as I have in that moment as a participant.

I appreciate what you say in terms of when you ask me, "You are bold enough to say that?" I don't consider that bold. I'm clear that many of my actions are considered bold. Very often I consider myself timid, as unusual as that may sound. (Laughing) I have the tendency to be timid. When I walk into a networking room and don't know anyone there, for the first 5 seconds I am timid. I don't walk up to people to say hello. I'm timid.

Last night we were coming back from being out and this stranger and guy walked up and said, "Who has been shopping?" I looked at him and noticed he had a bag from a department store. I said, "You." I would not have said that when he first walked up. I got timid. I know I'm quick. I can come up with something clever to say. He just kept talking, saying, "Thank you for supporting the economy. Women are always supporting the economy." We just kept conversing back and forth. This is unusual for me. I knew he wanted to play and I played. And, the reason I'm sharing is that for the first 5 seconds, I am timid. I didn't want him to say anything since I didn't know what I was going to say.

That's true for me. I tend to be timid, not bold. It doesn't last very long; however, I am timid. I've seen people walk right up and start talking. I'm not like that. I do know how to hold my own, and I'm not like that.

Answering your question as to what's an action I would not normally take? In the moments I am timid, I'm having a drama in those first 5 seconds. I'm in drama. "Oh my god what am I going to say. What if they talk to me? What if they don't? What if...?" What's the action I wouldn't normally take? The action I wouldn't normally take is to go and ask someone, "Is there someone sitting there?" or "Are you saving these seats for anyone?" That's the action to take to break the drama. Otherwise, I would find a chair where no one was around and I didn't have to talk to anyone. I could be by myself.

The little girl in me has the biggest fear that people are going to tell me to get lost and to go away. My little kid still thinks this. "Go away. Go away. We don't want to play with you." I don't know where this came from. I don't recall any children ever telling me to go away.

I do remember the experience of racial prejudice. That may be where that came from. I did experience racial prejudice.

I got beat up on my way to and from school. That's where I get the thought that someone is going to beat me up. Well, that's not true now. This is the challenge because the thought is there, "I might get beat up" or they might tell me to go away by saying, 'We don't want your kind here."

Intellectually I know that this thought is there.

Right now I'm back in the land where that all began, in Chicago. That energy is still here. The negativity and racial negativity is still here. That one I didn't make up. It is still here. I handle it and respond differently to it now. It has been an interesting experience to be back and handle that kind of racial arrogance and rejection.

I'm glad I've had years to work through the many layers of that. This is not a safe place for ethnicity. California is different. The only group there that I receive racial rejection from is the Hispanics. California was Hispanic for centuries. Once I understood that, I accepted it. I could accept it and have compassion. I understood where the anger came from and understood it was not personal.

Tuck: We have a lot of work to do culturally, don't we?

Carol McCall, PhD: The action I wouldn't normally take here in Chicago is not to take it personally. I remember how the realtors would intentionally gerrymander the neighborhoods so that ethnics could not live in certain areas. Whites would not sell you a home in certain areas. Deliberately, no whites would rent you an apartment in certain areas. That's the way it was set up here. And, with Chicago being the land of the gang mentality, the gangs are still here. It has been interesting to be back and to heal a lot of incompletions.

So, what is the action I would not normally take? The action I would not normally take is not to take it personally. It has nothing to do with me. It is simply to protect my own space. It's like saying what I did to the clerk behind the counter, "Slow down." And in my head the thoughts were, "You are not going to make me rush through ordering what I want to eat just because you are busy being busy. I'm going to enjoy selecting the food that I want to take home and participate in." I didn't want all of that energy in my food either.

This works. What's an action I wouldn't normally take? I say, Tuck, you are considered bold. When I hear your husband talk to me about how bold you are I have the thought you would find that surprising. I have the thought that you don't think you are bold.

Tuck: No, I would probably call that being mean.

Carol McCall, PhD: Yes, you confuse being bold with being mean. You call your Boldness mean. You are not mean. You are bold. Now, here's something I am being bold about. I shared with your brother the family systems information. He asked me about the four of you, you and your siblings.

The pairing was you and your brother, the oldest, and the other pairing was your older sister with your younger sister. In that moment I got clear how come your older sister has the issues she has with you. Hierarchically and in terms of the family system, that is not supposed to be the pairing.

For whatever reason, your brother paired with you. Since you were the child underneath your older sister, it was easier for her to take it out on you than it was for her to take it out on him. He is the surrogate father. He is the patriarch. He is the stand-in patriarch. He is the Daddy, the older son, the big boy. Children are attracted to the power structure.

The power structure was supposed to be your older brother and older sister. The underlings are you and your younger sister. It didn't work out that way. According to the family systems information, this is disruptive. Your older sister got knocked out of her legitimate place. She is the older sister. She is supposed to be the mother figure.

Tuck: Well, she is to my younger sister.

Carol McCall, PhD: No, she is supposed to be that for both you and your younger sister. You were lifted up, elevated by your brother to that place.

Tuck: So, where does my mother come in to the picture? My family will tell you that they believe that I was my mother's favorite, and that my brother could do no wrong, as the oldest and only boy. My younger sister called me a while back and shared a dream she had. In the course of her sharing she again brought up the concept that mother always liked me best. That belief is prevalent in our family system. And, it feels like the belief behind the pairing is that my brother and I are more alike. He enjoyed my life. We got along well together. My older sister from the earliest times I can remember took my younger sister under her wing and became her surrogate mother.

Carol McCall, PhD: That is the family dynamic. You asked me what about your mother? In the family systems information, your mother's energy was influenced from the perspective that your brother was the surrogate father, since he was the only boy and son. Your mother fell in place in terms of wherever he went she would go. That's what happens in family systems. Energetically if he went in a particular direction, so would she. That's how the systems work.

Tuck: Is that why when they would butt heads all hell would break loose?

Carol McCall, PhD: Yes, since that's not the dynamic understanding. The unspoken agreement is that we don't disagree in front of the children.

Tuck: So what is the way out of this family dynamic?

Carol McCall, PhD: The way out of it is to stay present. Take that one on in your family system, given that families are not present. You make choices about how you are going to be in your own system regardless of how you are treated. How are you going to be in your family system? There is a lot of stepping over to do, as in not giving energy to it.

One of the things I have consistently managed since being back in Chicago is staying away from my aunt who is the baby of the entire family. She is the last one living of that lineage. I stay away from her. For me, she is toxic. When I do call her, I tell her this is a business call or a happy birthday call, or I send her gifts. I will not put myself into her space when I speak to her. I don't want that toxicity. The whole time I have been here, I've been around her in huge groups. At most I will give her a quick hug. I stay away.

Tuck: I'm impressed that you can do that.

Carol McCall, PhD: I trained myself early on, Tuck. When I was giving my workshops early in my business, I would do some of them here in Chicago. I would call my family members to let them know I was in town. I wanted to inform all of them that I was present in the town and that I was giving this workshop. Also, I would most likely not see them. I would also give them a call from the airport as I was leaving to say good-bye and wish them well. I trained myself to do this early on.

When I was 18 or 19 I went to my last family gathering. I decided at that point not to go to one ever again. The last time I saw my grandmother was when my son was born. I was 25 years old. I had a swollen body, edema from retaining water. My grandmother kept telling me how fat I was. She would take

my son, talk to him, sing to him and then look at me and say, "My god girl you are fat." I remember saying back to her that if she said it to me again I would never be back to see her. Her response was again an affirmation that I was fat. When I left I told her that was the last time I would visit with her. She didn't believe me. I never saw her again until I attended her funeral. Now, my family knows that I do that. When I am done, I am done. I trained myself and my family members early.

Plus, in training as a therapist I was required to do therapy with my "role play" family. I wanted to get straight about how dysfunctional my family was. Once I got it and was through with all of my crying and drama, I got that families are ALL dysfunctional. The reason they are dysfunctional is from the perspective that children are held in a position in the family versus who they are and what their gifts and contributions are to the family. If you are the first born you are expected to do this. If you are the second or third child you are expected to do this. Families are dysfunctional. Then, we set up marriages the same way. They are dysfunctional.

It is very simple. I learned family dynamics from Virginia Satir. Then I have been doing a lot of follow up reading. I will share with you what I know of the family systems, particularly what I learned from Virginia Satir. It is fascinating once you understand family systems. Things get really clear.

According to Virginia Satir family systems information, I have two "only" children. My son is my first-born and my daughter is my baby. They are six years apart. Therefore for all practical purposes they are "only" children. I treat them that way. They are both first-borns. Yet, one is the first and the other is the baby. Both have a special place in my system from the perspective that I kept them away from my dysfunctional family system. They know about family systems. They understand it. They are both my "only" children. Even only children have a particular dynamic. There is an expectation as an only child. There is an expectation as the oldest child. There is an expectation as the baby.

Now put all that together, "only" child, oldest child, the baby and look at the dynamic. There is no wonder that they are leaders. No wonder they are up front about what works for them. They have big energy. This is from the combination of being the "only", the first and the combination of being the baby. That is big energy. In those positions they have an expectation that they will be treated as their mother treated them.

It all works. The final imprint for me was when I had to do therapy with my makeshift family. We had to role-play. They really played their roles well. The one thing I got from that was to keep my children away from the toxicity of my family, which I did, as much as possible. This was my Coach Action. I Stopped the Drama.

This concludes our conversation on The Nine Tools of Empowered Mindful Listening™. I am complete for now.

The Nine Tools of Empowered Mindful Listening™

IN PLAIN ENGLISH

1. Brevity: summation-a speaking style that makes the point concisely and clearly

2. Acknowledgement: a speaking style that enhances the communication in the form of contribution

3. Empowered Mindful Listening™: a listening style that "serves" both speaker and listener

4. Being Heard: a speaking and listening style that allows both speaker and listener to experience a complete exchange in the course of conversation

5. Boldness: a speaking style that is "true" to the moment, event, circumstance

6. Intuition: a "listening style" that is ALWAYS right

7. 99:1/MSU: a listening and speaking style that is ALWAYS something "made up" about the past or future

8. Completion: a listening and speaking style that allows the listener and speaker to move to the next event with a full focus/presence

9. Coach Action: a listening and speaking style that "stops-the-drama" in an interaction

LISTEN hard

PRACTICE presence,

PLAY with abandon,

LAUGH!

CHOOSE with no regret.

CONTINUE to learn.

APPRECIATE your friends.

DO what you love

LIVE AS IF THIS IS ALL THERE IS!

~Maryann Radmacher-Hershey~

GLOSSARY

The Human Design System is the Science of Differentiation. It shows each of us that we have a unique design and a specific purpose to fulfill while on Earth. Endless possibilities for individual uniqueness lie within our genetic matrix. There are millions of variations of human beings, yet each of us has a specific and unique Human Design configuration with a clear Strategy that effortlessly aligns us to our uniqueness.

The Gene Keys is a living transmission and activation code to guide you home, toward authenticity, self-acceptance and pure unbridled freedom. This activation code is your unique sacred geometry and Hologenetic pattern deeply encoded in your DNA.

Your **Hologenetic Profile** is the original blueprint that reveals your life story. It opens you fully to your own experience of life. Your **Hologenetic Profile** reveals 3 unique sequences of Gene Keys called The Golden Pathway.

The Golden Path is a master genetic sequence that allows you to contemplate the Gene Keys in a personalized way, with specific Gene Keys relating to certain areas of your life.

It is a Threefold Journey of spiritual awakening that has a powerful bearing on your individual higher purpose, your relationship patterns and family dynamics, your health, well-being, and financial prosperity.

Empowered Mindful Listening™: a listening style that "serves" both the speaker and listener. (Tool #3)

POW (Possibility of Woman) workshop (now called the Advanced Women's Intensive) - The 3-day Possibility of Woman Workshop recognizes that women, working in tandem with men, are powerful catalysts for social change.

The workshop is a vehicle through which women awaken to the powerful, untapped resource that they are and become pro-active in bringing their gifts to the world for the good of humankind.

This 3-day course provides individual and group practice in applying the seven tools of effective communication that enable women to break free from old, negative communication and negative health-producing habits and replace those habits with effective new ones.

This course addresses the challenges of being a woman in the 21st century and balancing the many roles a woman is required to play. The answer becomes clear in the Possibility of Woman 2.0 Workshop (aka the Advanced Women's Intensive) upon the discovery and recovery of the "core" of who she authentically is, irrespective of the roles she plays.

Empowered Mindful Listening™ **Workshop** (aka The Listening Course) is currently not being offered and is scheduled to be re-launched in 2020.

"Like their personal lives, women's history is fragmented, interrupted; a shadow of history of human beings whose existence has been shaped by the efforts and the demands of others" ~Elizabeth Janeway

ABOUT CAROL MCCALL, PHD

Carol McCall, PhD is the founder of the Institute for Global Listening and Communication. She has five decades of experience in communication and personal development as a successful educator, author, business executive, entrepreneur, trainer, lecturer, social psychologist and therapist. Since 1988, she has been recognized as one of the early pioneers and thought leaders in the coaching industry.

Author of the book, *Listen! There's A World Waiting To Be Heard*, and the soon to be released book *I Know You Hear Me. Are You Listening? The Empowerment of Mindful Listening*™: in early 2020. Dr. McCall is best known for her unique listening skills and her "laser" coaching ability that quickly moves people to turn their desires into commitment, action, results and profitability. She is expert in quickly assessing individual, couple and group dynamics with effective and practical solutions for challenging situations.

Listed as one of the top-rated speakers in the country and abroad, she has reached over 2 million people through her lectures, seminars, trainings, and book and tape series, now in MP3 format. She is a respected veteran leader, coach and trainer in both the MLM (multi-level marketing) and private business sectors since 1990.

Dr. McCall has delivered positive impact leadership training and communication solutions to such prestigious companies as Bayer Corporation, GE Capital, Amdahl and Unilever. She has also worked with educators, members of the court system, members of congress and the entertainment industry. Her international work has included Australia, Bermuda, Canada, England, Israel, Jamaica, Scotland, Singapore and Thailand.

In addition to creating and developing such renowned works as, The Listening Course, The Possibility of Woman (POW^{sm}) workshops, The Empowerment of Listening tape series and completing a co-executive production of a TV pilot with her daughter and business partner, Ana Floyd, PCC, Dr. McCall has also dedicated her life to developing some of the most stellar training programs in the world. One of her most effective programs is Life Development Coach in Communication (LDCC^{TM}) training program, which has been ongoing nationally and internationally since 1992.

Her goal is to assist individuals and organizations to develop systems that result in enhanced communication, improved job performance, healthier life styles and higher levels of life's satisfaction through efficiency, productivity and profitability.

For further information contact:

Dr. Carol McCall
1-(888)966-8339 X1
Email: drcarolmccall@gmail.com
drcarolmccall@listeningprofitsu.com
www.listeningprofitsu.com

ABOUT TUCK SELF

Tuck Self is the founder of SELF Empowerment Resources, LLC, a transformation coaching company that assists individuals and organizations with programs and services for wellness, emotional well-being, and personal and spiritual growth.

SELF Empowerment Resources Programs, Workshops and Retreats are a systematic approach that assists individuals and companies in learning to work in harmony with their divine vision and framework. Results create loving relationships, successful careers, healthy bodies, and happy lives. Programs combine accountability with principles that facilitate rapid personal discovery, development and spiritual growth. When you employ this knowledge and wisdom in your daily life you are empowered to design your life with unlimited possibilities!

Tuck has been developing personal fitness and individualized coaching programs, workshops and retreats for more than 15 years. She is a Certified Life Development Coach in Communication, a Certified Quantum Success Coach, a Certified Natural Law Coach, Fitness and Intuitive Eating Coach, and a Human Design Personal and Business Specialist.

Tuck is the author of *THE REBEL-UTION: A Woman's Rebelicious Guide to Freedom, Liberation and Bold Self-Expression.* She is a contributing author in the Amazon Best-Seller, *A*

Juicy Joyful Life: Inspiration from Women Who Have Found the Sweetness in Every Day, and *the Entrepreneur Success Stories: How Common People Achieve Uncommon Results.*

As a sought-after coach, writer, radio talk show host and inspirational speaker, Tuck's passion is to inspire others to live full out, and to boldly express their true selves with freedom, power and authenticity.

If you would like additional information contact:

Tuck Self
(803) 665-0847
Email: Tuck@TheRebelBelle.com
www.TheRebelBelle.com
YouTube: www.youtube.com/therebelbelle

CPSIA information can be obtained
at www.ICGtesting.com
Printed in the USA
LVHW051133290820
664260LV00002B/215

9 781641 840637